D1054723

Who Comes in the
Name of the Lord?

Who Comes in the Name of the Lord?

Jesus at the Margins

Harold J. Recinos

Abingdon Press
Nashville

WHO COMES IN THE NAME OF THE LORD?

Copyright © 1997 by Abingdon Press

All rights reserved.
No part of this work may be reproduced or transmitted in any form or by any means, electronic or mechanical, including photocopying and recording, or by any information storage or retrieval system, except as may be expressly permitted by the 1976 Copyright Act or in writing from the publisher. Requests for permission should be addressed to Abingdon Press, 201 Eighth Avenue South, P.O. Box 801, Nashville, TN 37202-0801.

Library of Congress Cataloging-in-Publication Data

Recinos, Harold J. (Harold Joseph), 1955-
    Who comes in the name of the Lord? : Jesus at the margins / Harold J. Recinos.
        p.   cm.
    Includes bibliographical references.
    ISBN: 0-687-01002-0 (pbk. : alk. paper)
    1. Church work with Hispanic Americans.   2. Protestant churches—United States.
3. Hispanic Americans—Religion.   I. Title.
BV4468.2.H57R43   1997
280'.4'08968073—dc21   97-39675
                                                                                                    CIP

Scripture quotations, unless otherwise indicated, are from the New Revised Standard Version Bible, copyright © 1989, by the Division of Christian Education of the National Council of the Churches of Christ in the United States of America.

Permission has been granted from EPICA for use of material previously published in *El Salvador: A Spring Whose Water Never Runs Dry.*

Text and figure "THE HOLISTIC NATURE OF ANTHROPOLOGY" from CULTURAL ANTHROPOLOGY by PAUL G. HIEBERT. Copyright © 1976 by Harper & Row, Publishers, Inc. Reprinted by permission of HarperCollins Publishers, Inc.

97 98 99 00 01 02 03 04 05 06—10 9 8 7 6 5 4 3 2 1

MANUFACTURED IN THE UNITED STATES OF AMERICA

To the Crucified People of El Salvador
Who Long for a Society of Peace with Justice

Contents

Life Goes On

I walked by the bleeding corner
today looking for the faces of
so many killed by others who

hide despair behind guns. my
eyes roamed the neighborhood
from the curve and noticed the

clocks in the bodegas not
telling time for the dead nor
those who will descend into

hell for their sake. the old
men who still live in the barrio
stare with disturbed eyes at the

young men on the corner who
they cannot understand but
fear. shadows stay eternally

on our streets while in them
we ponder a deep place inside
us where something has already

died. madness covers half
the soul of this barrio that
is home to a forgotten people

of this city where life goes
on never looking the other
way. . . .

Mainline Protestantism has been in a state of crisis regarding its cultural function in the United States. Mainline churches had for years enjoyed a privileged status in American society. They fulfilled the role of promoting cultural integration of individuals around a system of core beliefs, values, and practical behavior. They explained the meaning of U.S. social history in terms of a broader frame of reference rooted in biblical symbolism. Mainline Christians thought their interpretation of national identity and existence was indispensable to the social order. Nonetheless, now many mainline churches find themselves struggling to survive in a society that keeps them at the margin.

Since the Great Depression, mainline Protestant denominations have been experiencing more of their life at the edge of society as the government expanded its social functions to include areas deemed the church's unique domain. In a comprehensive study of American religion since World War II, Robert Wuthnow argues that with this expanding role of government the environment of American religion changed; moreover, as educational levels rose in society and various church groups shared more of a common culture, the significance of denominationalism declined.[1] Although conflicts between denominations have lessened and religious resources are mobilized interdenominationally, the mainline churches' marginality is accentuated by these new cultural conditions.

Between 1965 and 1990 mainline Protestant churches who were steadily losing members reported a total membership decline of one-fifth to one-third.[2] Members of my own United Methodist Church are raising questions about the future identity of their congregations and American religion. Mainline Protestant churches are facing declining attendance, economic crisis, and the possibility that in the future they will be less capable of culturally influencing a society that appears to act without any appeal to its dominant religious heritage. Indeed, the biblical theism that provided a common morality for national identity even during years of open conflict between Protestants, Catholics, and Jews is now an unstable meaning system.[3]

In part, membership decline in mainline Protestant churches has been explained by the forces of urbanization, secularization, and growing levels of mass education. Researchers have argued that these social factors produced cultural shifts in society that included the desacralization of the human order. The decline of religion, however, is never complete. People seek to understand their lives with reference to categories that transcend the boundaries of ordinary existence. Interestingly, conservative Christianity was gaining members in major cities despite the eroding impact of secularization. This suggests mainline Protestant church membership decline may be foremost explained by a decline of belief in the lives of members.[4]

For the most part, established culture bypasses church leaders on questions of meaning and moral guidance. This may seem to indicate that people now do not need a church to establish a sense of meaning in the world they inhabit. Americans seem more interested in diet and fitness books than the Bible. Many clergy persons from mainline Protestant churches are personally experiencing their denominations' marginalization in the wider society. Once treated as respected and influential members of local communities, ordained pastors now vocalize frustration over lost influence in community life. In a society lacking a universally accepted moral vision, mainline Protestant clergy and churches have gradually become just another set of minor actors.

Today, as the standard moral certitudes of mainline Christians enter into crisis stemming from the experience of marginality and competition with different moral interpretations of the gospel, barrio Christianity offers a fresh look at the meaning of faith in Jesus of Nazareth. It promises to renew belief in the church by calling Christians to enact the imperatives of the gospel in their personal and social lives. This book invites you to the barrio where the particular faith witness of the dehumanized poor and powerless reflects the liberating and empowering Spirit of God (Joel 2:28-29). Latino/Latina Christians largely forgotten by the mainline church and mainstream society are now articulating visions of a world based on the love and justice of God.

Latinos speak of a Jesus who pitches God's tent among the poor and calls for the renewal of the belief and practices of established Christianity. From the barrio the Jesus whose body is broken each day in the poor asks followers, "Who do you say that I am?" For years mainline Protestant churches have approached Jesus as the definitive answer for the human condition. In contemporary life where belief has declined and cultural diversity deabsolutizes meaning systems, Jesus approaches the world not so much as an answer to our confusion but as a hard-hitting question. I propose to take a fresh look at the question posed by Jesus to human beings by finding vital responses in the witness of those who live in the barrio.

Barrio people know what it means to live in a social reality structured in terms of suffering, violence, and death. The church will find Jesus in current social experience by looking at the barrio where poor, rejected, and socially and politically oppressed people explain the carpenter from Nazareth to the universal church. I believe that a new theology can be discovered by the mainstream church by walking the road to Emmaus that leads to the barrio. On that road Jesus will be rediscovered in the witness of people who have been turned into strangers by mainstream society. In the barrio, clarity about who Jesus is comes from breaking bread and entering into a new relationship with the strangers and outcasts (Luke 14:15; 24:35).

The church will find Jesus in the barrio. Latinos/Latinas invite mainline Christians to experience the gospel in the barrio where the racially despised and rejected live. Mainline Christians will learn to sing a new song about the God of the poor—strangers and outcasts in the witness of the barrio. For many mainline Christians who wonder about the future of their churches, the barrio has a special word of address. Barrio Christianity says the future does not include a new culture and religion synthesis on conservative ground. Neither does the future look more contentious with mainline denominations competing against other Christian and secular groups for the moral center in society. Membership decline is also not to determine the meaning of the church.

By reading the Bible from the perspective of the barrio, the mainline church will rise to an existence more basic than any now imagined. Reading the Bible from the perspective of the barrio means recognizing that God has already prepared an identity and a future for mainline Christians in society. Mainline Christians must never forget that Paul reminds believers that God-in-Christ begins the church with despised, lowly, powerless, and rejected humanity (1 Cor. 1:26-29). The church's identity, future, and place in the world is with those who count for nothing. God who takes the side of utterly rejected human beings invites culturally marginal mainline Protestant churches to the world of the rejected—the barrio.

Notes

1. Robert Wuthnow, *The Restructuring of American Religion* (Princeton, N.J.: Princeton University Press, 1988).
2. Benton Johnson, Dean R. Hoge, and Donald A. Luidens, "Mainline Churches: The Real Reason for Decline," *First Things* 31 (March 1993), p. 13.
3. See especially James Davison Hunter "American Protestantism: Sorting Out the Present, Looking Toward the Future," *This World* 17 (spring 1987), pp. 53-76.
4. See Johnson, Hoge, and Luidens, "Mainline Churches: The Real Reason for Decline," pp. 13-18.

Chapter One

The Struggle for National Identity

Burning in Heaven

they burn Black churches
again denying God through
a violence that only fools

all manner of humanity
in their hearts. from a fire
in a bush that never lost

its life God spoke to
Moses of freedom for
all humanity—enslaved.

from the ashes of Black
churches achieved by the
terror of a racist America

God recites bold words of
overcoming. out of fires
of hate that crucify the

certain beauty of God's
own creation redemption
draws near to make each

day a celebrated mixture of
people who see no faces made
in hate nor know endless

crying. . . .

The breakup in the 1960s of the historic Judeo-Christian theism resulted in a worldview shift in America that resulted in a reorientation toward a greater awareness of cultural and religious pluralism. During this period persons began to show a keen interest in the human potential movements, secular philosophies, and emerging forms of Eastern spirituality.[1] By the 1980s, mainline Protestant churches were forced to examine trends that showed young adults dropping out of the church and leaving behind aging congregations with dim prospects of future life. Mainline Protestant churches are now facing membership decline and are trying to redefine their identity and influence in national life; yet, national life reflects a new pluralism defined by competing moral visions.[2]

Sociologist James Davison Hunter argues that religious communities with different moral outlooks are currently involved in a culture war over defining American national identity and social reality.[3] Important divisions between religious communities no longer center on theological, ecclesiastical, regional, class, and racial/ethnic contrasts. Rising levels of education and social mobility have created a largely identical religious and cultural experience for members of most denominations.[4] Cultural and religious pluralism is now expressed in divisions of another kind. Different moral visions are presently promoted by particular groups meaning to institutionalize their interpretation of national identity and the dominant symbols of shared culture.

Consequently, in the United States, opposing moral outlooks decide the social divisions informing the political disagreements of religious and cultural groups. Who are the contending parties? According to Hunter, oppositional worldviews in national religious life issue forth as polarizing tendencies expressed as an impulse toward orthodoxy and an impulse toward progressivism.[5] On one side is an orthodox alliance that views moral authority as objective, unchanging, and transcending the social order. On the other side stands a progressivist alliance whose members locate moral authority in modern suppositions of truth. Truth is not unchanging and above culture; instead, progressivists see it as a cumulative product of historical change open to correction.[6]

Not surprisingly, a religious culture that is polarized into orthodox and progressive communities of moral understanding decides important social issues in the public square. This is evidenced when vocal elites largely connected to special-interest groups mobilize social and political hostility in the function of serving their views in the conflicted arena of shared cultural space.[7] For instance, between the 1950s and the 1980s conflict on social issues related to the civil rights struggle, the Vietnam War, global poverty, women's rights, gay and lesbian rights, abortion, the nuclear family, alternative lifestyles, nuclear arms and energy, capitalism, and U.S. foreign policy in Central America manifested opposing moral visions in American religion.[8]

Basically, the culture conflict between the orthodox and progressives is about controlling the symbols and meaning of national identity. For instance, in the 1980s opposing moral visions framed the United States's role in Central American civil wars. The orthodox alliance interpreted the U.S. role in Central America as both an extension of the divine origin of "America" and a defense of the biblically mandated system of free enterprise, democratic government, and ownership of property. Meanwhile, progressivists who struggled to gain control of America's symbol system interpreted the principles of Americanism as the concern for social justice. For them national identity meant advocating an end to U.S. support for political oppression in Central America.[9]

In the United States, cultural conflict is mostly located in the institutional structures of American culture such as the family, popular media, education, law, and politics.[10] Indeed, the news media have indicated how culture wars are fought over the meaning of the family, abortion, use of public funds for the arts, gay and lesbian rights,

Supreme Court decisions regarding school prayer and reproductive rights, the symbolic meaning of political candidates, and multiculturalism in the curriculum of public schools. Cultural meaning and a sense of social order for individuals are established by each side of the cultural divide by vocal leaders who marshal social forces that seek to have their moral outlook become the established standard for society.

Until recently, the culture wars were largely confined to the public discourse of politicized proponents of adversarial moral and ideological camps. Subdivisions of the orthodox alliance, however, have engaged in physical violence. For instance, in December of 1994 a former Presbyterian minister, Paul Hill, was convicted of gunning down an abortion clinic doctor and his bodyguard. And who can forget the federal building bombing in Oklahoma City? Will the future bring more physical violence? Clearly, struggles over the meaning of the public symbols of national life are important; yet, Hunter's discussion requires more serious consideration of the role of race, ethnicity, and empire-building in the formation of national identity in the United States.

Race and Empire-Building

Today, the subject of racism is on American minds and it is discussed as both the special interests of people of color and "white-male bashing." Still, racially oppressed people tell members of the larger society that the cultural invention of race—linked to the European expansion into Asia, Africa, and Latin America—resulted in the social denial and inhumane economic exploitation of non-White people. European conquest and settlement meant about seventy million indigenous people and forty million Africans were slaughtered to meet the needs of North Atlantic economic expansionism.[11] The concept of race is linked to the conquest project of European societies in the New World and the idea of race is fundamental to identity formation in the United States.

Unquestionably, five hundred years ago racially drawn distinctions between White and non-White groups in society appeared in the agonized cry of the racially despised. People of color were the fuel used to give rise to the capitalist world system that now envelops most societies on earth. Race served to determine who should have access to wealth, privilege, respect, and power and who should not. Race decided who was crucified. As Christianity interpreted the mission of the church from the perspective of the powerful, it too declared that conquest and the exploitation of non-White peoples were the will of God. Yet Jesus says the people who are abused and oppressed on the basis of their color require justice and the respect of their human rights.

Mainline Protestant churches need to deal honestly with the history of American religion that deplorably harmonized the gospel with a racist and conquest-oriented project of nation-building. Mainline Protestants must question the regular relationship between Christianity and American national identity. One missiologist, the late Orlando Costas, found little evidence of true Christianity in a social project that was established on the grounds of conquest, racism, classism, sexism, and deism. True Christian values would discourage people from building a nuclear arsenal, promoting ecological destruction, and socially neglecting the weak, the poor, and children; indeed, the true church looks for the Crucified God who is with the poor and racially despised.[12]

To be sure, the God crucified each day by the racial oppression experienced by people of color bids the church to examine its cultural history. Such a reflection will enable the church to look at the Cross as exposing God within the history of people whose cries and pain reveal even now how they are violated by racist behavior and made outcasts of society. Why are people crucified on the basis of their race? Let us first find an answer by briefly examining the origin and evolution of racism as a worldview. That history forms the proper context of individual and collective identity in our society and church. Such a discussion will clarify the context of my barrio Christology and theology of the Cross to be explored in the next two chapters.

Racism As a Worldview

In North America human differences have largely come to be expressed in the idiom of race. People attribute racial identities to themselves and to others because they believe it is a natural order of things. But the idea of race is not something that objectively exists in the world waiting simply to be confirmed by the empirical sciences.[13] More to the point, race is a cultural category that organizes people's perceptions of one another into racially distinct and exclusive groups. Race is an invention of European cultures that served the political purposes of social, economic, and territorial domination. This cultural invention refers less to physical variation and more to culturally based perceptions and interpretations of human differences.[14]

Class, language, religion, customs, sex, and many other culturally established interpretations have been used to account for human variation. So what is the origin and effect of the idea of race? Why is the idea of race the most ubiquitous aspect of our daily life? The racial worldview was culturally constructed particularly in the period of European New World expansionism, the encountering of non-European populations, and the creation of slavery.[15] Race was an ideological and organizing principle of the expansion, conquest, exploitation, and enslavement unleashed in Western history some five hundred years ago. Thus, the historical roots of racism are decidedly in the context of European conquest, colonization, and capitalist development.

By the fifteenth century, the term race appears in the language of Europeans who ventured into the New World and had contact with diverse cultural groups. In the language of the French, Portuguese, Spanish, Italian, German, Dutch, and English colonial empires the concept of race is used to classify human beings into discrete and unequal groups.[16] It was not long before the idea of race supplanted other constructs of symbolic identity such as class, gender, age, religion, language, ethnic group membership, and culture. Race was nothing less than a socially symbolic rule for distributing status, power, and wealth to individuals and groups. From the cultural standpoint, the idea of race guided the norms of social interaction.

Whites who occupied North America between the late-sixteenth and eighteenth centuries were enthralled by the promise of economic progress in the New World. Their European morality and cultural orientation regulated the field of social and material relations in the

New World. Specifically, the English colonists enacted the cultural theme of "possessive individualism" that linked human freedom with private property. Not only did a racial worldview justify the despoiling economic practices and legal conventions of Europeans in the New World, but it promoted a custom of domination whose effect was African enslavement and Native American genocide and land dispossession.

Racism is a worldview. Essentially, a worldview is a comprehensive way of seeing and interpreting social reality and human interaction in it. The enslavement of Black and Native American humanity served to institutionalize the racial worldview in the Americas. As a worldview, racism conveys that biologically distinct groups are inherently unequal. That the racial worldview whose roots are especially found in the enslavement of Africans was, over time, culturally augmented to include other non-White people is not surprising. Rules of behavior, inequality, exploitation, and social class divisions are assigned by racism. Anthropologist Audrey Smedley identifies five ideological ingredients in the racial worldview that are now diagnostically useful.[17]

Smedley argues that the racial worldview first assumes that human groups are classified into distinct and exclusive biological beings. Essentially, this means that on the basis of appearances, ideas about differences in social behavior are constructed. Second, the impressions formed about visible group differences are ranked on a superior-inferior continuum. Such a system of ranking introduces a value system of inequality into society. Third, outer physical features are linked to such inner factors as mental, temperamental, moral, and affectional qualities. Thus, traits attributable to culture are allocated a biological origin.

Fourth, the racial worldview assumes then that cognition, social rank, and culture are also biologically inherited features of human life. In the logic of this belief people physically inherit their features, intellectual power, moral nature, and cultural system of affection, belief, and behavior. The fifth ingredient to the racial worldview is the idea that each race was uniquely created by God who imputed differences that are fixed and unalterable. This means that since biophysical variation was itself sanctioned by ultimate reality, institutions based on a racist ethos are legitimate. Hence, Blacks and other non-White persons can be treated as "less than human" in a world created by God for an ostensibly superior White humanity.

Racism is today pervasive in the social practices and institutions of the United States. Race is a symbolic boundary that assures that a social distance is kept between different groups. In North America racism determines residential patterns, quality of education, perceptions of the city and racial/ethnic youth behavior, marriage rules, formal and informal alliances, and church membership. The racial worldview is regularly reflected in cultural forms such as the theater, film, music, art, law, scientific research, national holidays, public education, and leisure activities.[18] People simply carry in their heads racist rules for daily interaction with others presumed exclusively different from themselves.

In North America racism justified hereditary slavery for three centuries and promoted segregation in the South for even longer than that. It also backed the belief that God endorsed slavery and had chosen Whites to Christianize and civilize the so-called "heathen" people of the new world.[19] It explains why English slave ships arrived on the shores of North America with Black humanity in chains who bore names like Jesus of Lubeck and John the Baptist. It elucidates why New England Puritans believed that Indian deaths cleared the way for them to take possession of the land.[20] The vicious treatment of Native Americans and enslaved Africans in the early period of this nation comes as no surprise when seen as a feature of a racist ideology backed by religion.

The racial worldview that partly backed American wars of territorial expansion cast Latinos into a segregated, racially despised, and cheap labor force. Racism now tells Whites to call Mexicans and other Latinos freeloaders, greasers, spiks, wetbacks, stupid, or illegal aliens. The racial worldview clearly justified Latino lynchings in the Southwest during the period of American expansionism just as today this worldview justifies pavement lynchings by the police in cities across the nation. The racial worldview is evidenced in the English-only movement, proposition 187 that denies services to the undocumented immigrant, and the consistent negative images of Latinos projected by the media. Indeed, many feel that Latinos are the most negatively imaged group in the media and in film in the States.

Race is also not a static system of social meaning. Larger social forces played a significant role in determining the content and meaning of the racial worldview in the United States. In other words, the idea of race is constantly being shaped and reshaped by everyday social, economic, political, and cultural struggles of identity.[21] For instance, Black Christianity as a political movement challenged the racist ethos of White society as it articulated the message of the Bible. Black Christians who were crucified by the practices of racist society fought for their rights. Spurred by belief in a Savior who was killed by oppressive religious and political forces, the subversive memory of Jesus was incarnated in the Black struggle for freedom and justice.[22]

At the time of the civil rights struggle, Black religion as an opiate of the masses was condemned by prophetic church leaders. For instance, Martin Luther King Jr. voiced a bold sense of religious struggle that contested the social meaning of race and inequality in White society. Any religious tradition claiming to save souls was also required to confront the crippling conditions of an unjust economy and the life-denying slums. In other words, religion that was only otherworldly in focus, treating real unjust suffering as unimportant was a "dry-as-dust religion."[23] Beginning with race, King demanded the moral reorganization of White society in light of God's Word concerning the equality of all persons.

Between the 1950s and 1960s African Americans, Latinos, Asians, and Native Americans mobilized politically to transform the racial worldview of the United States. With politicized identities, people of color—denigrated by the established racial worldview and suffering the pain of economic and social exploitation—evolved a renewed sense of activism and political self-identity.[24] In the racial movements of the time, both in and outside of the church, people of color were not trying to find a way to live comfortably in a racist society. Blacks, Latinos, Asians, and Native Americans found ways to mobilize economic, political, spiritual, and cultural resources for the sole purpose of eradicating racial oppression and installing a more human social and economic order.

Nevertheless, there was a reaction to such a vision of society in the United States. In the 1980s, the White political right's moral outlook and identity construction even reached the White House. Subdivisions of conservative White society recaptured political power and condemned the official and institutionalized practices especially favoring people of color. White males began to articulate a sense of reverse discrimination.[25] With the cultural meaning of whiteness destabilized by racial movements for justice, the vocal elite of conservative think tanks and the Religious Right stormed the public square. Hoping to repossess the "white man's terrain," cultural conservatives criticized government enforcement of laws and social programs benefiting people of color.[26]

Although overt racism was largely inhibited due to the civil rights gains of earlier years, in the 1980s the racial worldview continued to operate in the United States in more subtle ways. New ways were found to attack the legally sponsored political strength of racial and powerless ethnic groups. For instance, busing was viewed as an attack on family rights, multiculturalism was opposed in the form of textbook censorship favoring "traditional family and lifestyles." When government or businesses enacted affirmative action and other programs excluding benefits to White males, reverse discrimination was declared.[27] The U.S. Civil Rights Commission under Ronald Reagan and George Bush supported and defended claims of reverse discrimination.

The Invisible Cage

Racism is the product of a cultural history that gets rehearsed in everyday practices in the arena of social relationships and public discourse. Americans live in an invisible cage of racism, and their social field of perception is immersed in a racial worldview.[28] In the early 1990s a major event in urban America manifested how the racial perception of White society is structured well in advance to sinisterly and criminally interpret people of color. In March 1991, the American public saw on network television video representation of White Los Angeles police officers brutally beating a young Black man named Rodney King. The racist epistemology of White society socially reconstructed Rodney King into an agent of violence.[29]

For instance, King was kicked, blasted with stun guns, and struck some fifty-six times. He suffered a split lip, his leg, eye socket, and cheekbone were broken, and he sustained nine skull fractures.[30] The interpretive framework of racism imposed a *reading* on the video evidence and Rodney King was portrayed as a "dangerous Black body" endangering police officers.[31] Four White police officers stood trial in Simi Valley for the beating of this twenty-five-year-old Black man. Only two people of color—one Asian and one Latino—served on the jury. The jurors acquitted the four police officers, convinced by defense attorneys that King was rightly struck down by the officers. Still, people of color saw King's bludgeoning and the acquittal as an incident in the long history of racism in the States.

Certainly, White racism was legitimated by the legal process, and a young Black man was silenced by the system. The acquittal of the White police officers confirmed the reading that King was the agent of his own beating. A part of urban America contested such a social construction of White domination. Between April 30 and May 2, 1992, a social explosion overcame Los Angeles even as the nation geared for a presidential campaign that surely would have to address issues of race and urban disintegration.[32] In Los Angeles, people of color, who stand on the other side of racial domination, used a weapon of the weak—the power to disrupt.[33] The most neglected segments of American society then set a limit on the prolongation of State enforced suffering.[34]

The Los Angeles uprising strongly contested larger structures of racial domination that mostly blame Blacks and Latinos for poverty, crime, and national economic decline. It was mostly African Americans and Latinos who sent a message back to the state that critiqued both the neoconservative and pragmatic liberal readings of the problems of the ghetto and barrio. The L.A. rebellion warned that the problems at the margins of society neither result from the failures of state activity nor evidence a defective morality of the poor. Instead, the uprising stems from state neglect and support for regressive economic restructuring resulting in underfunding for public education, a loss of low-skilled jobs, and the growth of drug economies in the barrios and ghettos.[35]

In the 1990s, urban rebellion did more than move toward the Left the concerns of the civil rights movement.[36] For instance, the so-called Rodney King riots turned ordinary Americans across the nation and people around the world into listeners of the loud cry of the barrio. What people heard was not the solitary cry of Black America; instead, it was the combined voices of a multiracial community of a city defined by cultural diversity, historical hispanicization, and ongoing plant closings fueling economic decline and racial antagonism. The Los Angeles riot also challenged and contradicted the biologically based biracial structure operative in American society. Hence, a fundamental aspect of race relations and national identity in the United States was questioned.

The Witness

I've come back to the
city weeping old tears
provided by the shattered

lives miracles ignore.
I see churches that
did not flee the horror

of this ghetto still
conjuring hope for all
the people who yearn for

a God who does not shorten
days nor answer prayers
with a colossal silence.

I walked past the finest
business on the block
where Abuelita* was laid

in a coffin made of
the lightest wood
our money could buy

aware of her last words
warning against every life
in the neighborhood becoming

a grave. then, I pause before
the mural painted on the wall
of a building at the end of

the street to read the
names of friends now dead
to this glass world in the

South Bronx.

* Abuelita: Grandmother

Not Just Black and White

The Los Angeles uprising did reveal that the cultural system of the United States constructs racial identity primarily in terms of a biologically based biracial structure.[37] For instance, mainstream journalism designated the Los Angeles "riots" a Black protest. Yet the Los Angeles uprising negated Black and White categories of racial meaning. Although official readings made their presence socially invisible, racial groups other than Black and White were involved or victimized during the social explosion. Korean shop owners who were portrayed in the liberal press as racists and vigilantes mostly watched their stores get looted and burned.[38] Moreover, 40 percent of the businesses burned were owned by Latinos.

Blackness and whiteness are culturally constituted symbols that regulate racial meaning in the States. As defining categories they produce, modify, and constrain perceptions of race and typically push more institutionally and politically powerless racial groups into invisibility and silence. Because these regulative symbols of racial discourse interpreted the Los Angeles riot as an episode in the history of Black and White race relations, the implicit protest language of unheard racial ethnic peoples such as Latinos and Asians was made unintelligible. Specifically, the conclusions of dominant culture regarding what took place in Los Angeles manifested the relative powerlessness of Latinos and Asians who are shut out of the imagined established community.

The racial epistemology that permeates national identity in the States clearly gives rise to an ideology that distinctly omits close examination of the oppressed suffering of Latinos and other racially distinct groups. For instance, Latino existence was excluded from society when the institutionalized biracial gaze caused most Americans to fail to observe that Latinos constitute about 51 percent of South Central Los Angeles residents; moreover, Latinos made up about one-third of those arrested and one-third of the fifty-eight deaths. Indeed, police chief Daryl Gates publicly blamed "illegal aliens" for most of the looting of stores. America's biracially structured social system typically dismisses the existence and historical experience of Latinos.

It is not surprising that members of both Black and White society failed to notice publicly that between 1975 and 1980 Los Angeles County police alone killed a total of thirty-five Latinos.[39] Latino "pavement lynchings" by the police are daily occurrences that are customarily not reported in the mass media or regularly condemned by recognized civil rights organizations. In 1990 in New York City, Puerto Ricans outpaced all other groups suspiciously killed by the police. Latino civil rights organizations dealing with these concerns rarely gain a hearing in the national press. Religious organizations whose views are conditioned by a biracial understanding of society also rarely discuss or take action against Latino civil and human rights violations in America.

Creating a new language of racial discourse for the American national identity requires recognition that race matters in more than Black and White.[40] Surely, American national identity must overhaul its outdated racial understanding that influences public institutions to adjust themselves largely to Black and White concerns. For instance, a largely biracial standard of perception is clearly at work in the way the Smithsonian Institution, an important cultural establishment for shaping and amending national identity in the States, represents Americans to the public. In 1993, twenty-six million people visited the Smithsonian Institution-run museums whose purpose it is to elevate and distribute knowledge about cultural identity in America.

Compared to the progress made by African Americans in being represented by the Smithsonian Institution, Latinos are standing still. They have largely been excluded from the representational, research, and educational concerns of the Smithsonian Institution.[41] Although Latinos have roots dating back to the early sixteenth century in what is now the United States, exclusion from the Smithsonian Institution contributes to the incorrect perception that very little has been contributed by Latinos to national history, cultural identity formation, social development, and economic evolution. Latino exclusion has been quite thorough, encompassing the areas of staffing, governance, programming, exhibits, and collections.[42]

To be sure, biracially framed practical decisions in education, employment, cultural representation, and politics mostly grants fewer rights and secures less power for Latinos in the States. Exclusion means Latino political disempowerment, and less access to jobs, education, social services, and defense of civil rights. Understanding America in terms other than Black and White means realizing that nearly 60 percent of Puerto Rican children grow up poor and that six of every ten Latino families are among the poorest two-fifths of the national population.[43] A new set of eyes will help Black and White Americans see that Latinos are the most discriminated group in housing markets and the workers most exposed to the worst job hazards.[44]

Breaking out of the established biracial understanding of identity in American society also results in a decisive break with the prevailing ideology that turns all Latinos into "unwanted foreigners." In other words, a biracially understood national identity both negates the Latino contribution to national life as well as molds local beliefs that negatively define Latinos as "illegal aliens" or "outsiders" deserving exclusion from the established community. Only a language of racial discourse that organizes social perceptions on the basis of the real ethnic diversity of American society leads to an awareness that life together is a rich mosaic of cultures, each eager for recognition.

Interestingly, in 1877, Latino social invisibility and removal from the American fabric was recognized by the American poet Walt Whitman. He lamented that one day Latino contributions to national identity would remain largely unrecorded by dominant culture and unknown to most citizens.[45] Demographic shifts tell yet another story. Latinos will shortly become the largest racial/ethnic group in the nation. Already Latinos are the racial/ethnic majority in San Francisco and Pasadena, Calif.; Homestead, Kissimmee, and Lake Worth, Fla.; Arlington, Va.; Las Vegas, Nev.; Lynn, Mass.; Providence, R.I.; Rockville, Md.; Waukegan, Ill.; Central Islip and Long Beach on Long Island; Yonkers, N.Y.; Paterson and Woodbridge, N.J.; and Danbury and Waterbury, Conn.[46]

Latinos have influenced American national identity in the areas of music, language, sports, cuisine, and entertainment. American English, in particular, draws on Latino words that were already naming social reality and natural objects prior to the arrival of English-speaking colonists. Familiar examples of the Latino influence on English are words like cantina, bronco, amigo, adios, coyote, gringo, guerrilla, hacienda, hurricane, junta, loco, maize, canyon, plaza, rio, rodeo, patio, sierra, and vista. An observant American will note that many of the nation's states, cities, towns, rivers, mountains, deserts, wildlife, and plants have Spanish names.[47] In other words, American English already speaks in Spanish.

Familiar Latino actors who have influenced U.S. cultural life include Academy Award winners José Ferrer and Rita Moreno.[48] Others are Ricardo Montalban, Fernando Lamas, Chita Rivera, and Raul Julia. Musicians like Willie Colon, Eddie Palmiere, Celia Cruz, Ray Barreto, and Tito Puente have introduced Latino rhythms—such as the mambo, tango, bossa nova, salsa, rumba, or the ever-popular bamba—into American music. Americans are familiar with Ritchie

Valens, Joan Baez, Gloria Estefan, Jon Secada, Trini Lopez, José Feliciano, and Julio Iglesias.[49] Americans are learning of Latino writers from anthologies that reflect Latino life in the States.[50] Latinos constitute 20 percent of the Major League Baseball players and have helped popularize soccer in the States.[51]

Equal in God's Eye

Because life in the States is tumbling toward a great void of social conflict, Americans who are busy engaging in interchurch and secular disputes regarding who possesses the correct interpretation of ultimate truth and national identity need to find a way to dialogue. Americans must finally question the established cultural values reflected in social behavior that excludes the people of the barrio from national identity. More than ever, this means finding the meaning of national identity in the particularity and fullness of the historical experience of all the people who make up American society. The truth of American society is to be found in the particularity of various cultures.

Christians must discard that language that conserves a biologically based biracial social structure and begin speaking a new language of community rooted in the details of American racial histories. The racial and ethnic diversity of America means African American and White Christians are not allowed to ignore nor forget the other ways of being in America. Culturally established Americans[52] must face other cultural and racial viewpoints in their contrast and divergence. Because America is a multicultural and multiracial society, American Christians can no longer evade weighing the meaning of the gospel and national identity in the context of cultural difference.

Hence, articulating a national identity means engaging in a mutual interpretation of racially constructed historical experience. In this regard, Latinos will continually invite members of established culture to march to the periphery of history where Latinas challenge the powerful in the imagination of their hearts and Jesus raises the barrio to be an instrument of liberation from multicultural and multiracial blindness. Latinos will not allow the biracial social structure to ignore the stench of death pervading the barrio and Latin American village streets. Latinos cannot move toward genuine dialogue on matters of racial experience and the meaning of national identity unless they are counted among those who belong.

Positive dialogue on the Latino role in national identity formation will only result from deposing interracial social alienation and White racism. Social indifference or active opposition to the Latino community by groups empowered by the biracial norms of American society can only mean that attempts to establish movements of interracial solidarity that existed during periods in the labor movement and civil rights era will be severely restricted.[53] As racialist norms influence the battle to set standards for national identity, the church needs to remind Americans that cultural and ethnic diversity is the foundation of society in the United States.

Surely, America's multicultural and racially diverse history on the issue of national identity suggests that no one can unreflectively say Latinos do not belong; yet, Proposition 187 that was passed in California in November 1994 makes such an assertion. Mostly, the children of European immigrants have argued that undocumented Latino/Latina immigrants come to the United States to receive welfare and put pressure on social services. Proposition 187 denies public, medical, and educational services to so-called "illegal immigrants." Healthcare providers and school officials are expected to report "illegal aliens" to the Immigration and Naturalization Service (INS). Most of the nation's "illegal immigrants" are Latino. This means many non-foreign born Latinos will likely get reported as well.

Proposition 187 is blamed for the death of Julio Cano, a fifteen-year-old child whose parents were "illegal immigrants" from Mexico. Julio died of heart complications resulting from a bacterial infection brought on by acute leukemia. Julio's parents were denied nonemergency medical services once before in California. With the passage of Proposition 187 they did not take their ill son to the hospital because they feared authorities would report them to the INS, resulting in deportation.[54] Proposition 187 could not have passed without the Mexican American and Black vote. If racial and cultural diversity are kept from defining the national identity by more established groups, we are truly left to wander in a dehumanizing forest.

Clearly, Black/White relations in North America will not be the basis for defining national identity into the next century. Quite simply, American society reflects changes that indicate that over the next fifty years 32 percent of the national population will be Latino, Native American, and Asian/Pacific American. Nearly one-third of North American society will be represented by racial/ethnic people of color; furthermore, Latinos will be the majority group of racial/ethnic people of color. The social experiences and histories of America's various people of color both indisputably challenge Black/White models of race and require a new look at the meaning of national identity. Racial/ethnic people's common interests also beg for a multiracial paradigm of national identity.

American Christians will draw new insight by thinking of the meaning of national identity in terms that are neither Black nor White. I propose a theology of marginality for mainline Christians to understand the cross of oppression carried by racial/ethnic people. Such a theology teaches the church that God is comprehended in the life of crucified people of color. People of color who have been marginalized and crucified by White racist practices are agents of a new vision of humanity. In particular, Latinos are speaking of a Jesus who pitches God's tent among them and calls for the renewal of belief and practices in Christianity. Through disregarded Latinos, who are judged by society to be racially inferior and "illegal aliens," Jesus asks "Who do you say that I am?"

Notes

1. See especially Wade Clark Roof and William McKinney, *American Mainline Religion* (New Brunswick, N.J.: Rutgers University Press, 1992), pp. 11-12.
2. See James Davison Hunter, *Culture Wars: The Struggle to Define America* (New York: Basic Books, 1991).
3. See especially Hunter, *Culture Wars: The Struggle to Define America.*
4. See Robert Wuthnow, *The Restructuring of American Religion* (Princeton, N.J.: Princeton University Press, 1988).
5. Hunter, *Culture Wars*, p. 43.
6. Ibid., chapter 4.
7. Ibid., p. 42.

8. James Davison Hunter, "American Protestantism: Sorting Out the Present, Looking Toward the Future," *This World* 17 (spring 1987), p. 64.

9. Hunter, *Culture Wars,* pp. 108-16.

10. Ibid., part 4.

11. Harold Recinos, *Hear the Cry! A Latino Pastor Challenges the Church* (Philadelphia: Westminster Press, 1989), p. 74.

12. Orlando Costas, *Christ Outside the Gate* (Maryknoll, N.Y.: Orbis Books, 1982).

13. See especially Audrey Smedley, *Race in North America: Origin and Evolution of a Worldview* (Boulder, Col.: Westview Press, 1993).

14. Ibid.

15. Ibid., p. 14.

16. Ibid., pp. 36-40.

17. Ibid., p. 27.

18. Ibid., p. 21.

19. Harold Recinos, *Jesus Weeps: Global Encounters on Our Doorstep* (Nashville: Abingdon Press, 1992).

20. See Gary B. Nash, "Red, White and Black: The Origins of Racism in Colonial America," in *The Origins of American Slavery and Racism,* ed. D. Noel (Columbus, Oh.: Charles E. Merrill, 1972).

21. See especially Michael Omi and Howard Winant, *Racial Formation in the United States: From the 1960s to the 1980s* (New York: Routledge, 1986).

22. Harold Recinos, *Jesus Weeps: Global Encounters on Our Doorstep* (Nashville: Abingdon Press, 1992), chapter 4.

23. As quoted in Aldon Morris, *The Origins of the Civil Rights Movement: Black Communities Organizing for Change* (New York: Free Press, 1984), p. 97.

24. See Omi and Winant, *Racial Formation in the United States.*

25. Ibid., p. 114.

26. Ibid., pp. 114-23.

27. Ibid., pp. 125-26.

28. Judith Butler, "Endangered/Endangering: Schematic Racism and White Paranoia" in *Reading Rodney King, Reading Urban Uprising,* ed. Robert Gooding-Williams (New York: Routledge, 1993), p. 15.

29. Ibid., p. 16.

30. Houston A. Baker, "Scene . . . Not Heard" in *Reading Rodney King, Reading Urban Uprising,* ed. Robert Gooding-Williams (New York: Routledge, 1993), p. 42.

31. Butler, "Endangered/Endangering: Schematic Racism and White Paranoia," p. 17.

32. Michael Omi and Howard Winant, "The Los Angeles 'Race Riot' and Contemporary U.S. Politics," in *Reading Rodney King, Reading Urban Uprising,* ed., Robert Gooding-Williams (New York: Routledge, 1993), p. 99.

33. Ibid.

34. Ibid., p. 100.

35. Omi and Winant, "The Los Angeles 'Race Riot' and Contemporary U.S. Politics," pp. 97-114.

36. Aldon Morris, "Centuries of Black Protest: Its Significance for America and the World" in *Race in America: The Struggle for Equality,* ed., Herbert Hill and James E. Jones, Jr. (Madison, Wis.: University of Wisconsin Press, 1993), pp. 52-53.

37. The cultural otherness of Latinos partly issues forth from the legacy of Protestant English culture. The institutionalization of Protestant English culture facilitated a dualist conceptualization of race in North America that included the denial and exclusion of multiracial identities as typified by most Latinos. The English abhorrence for and fear of racial admixture partly explains why cultural discourse represented as categories of identity Black and White social parties. In other words, Americans were either Black or White, but certainly not a person of mixed ancestry such as Native American, Spanish, and African.

38. Sumi K. Cho, "Korean Americans vs. African Americans: Conflict and Construction" in *Reading Rodney King, Reading Urban Uprising,* ed., Robert Gooding-Williams (New York: Routledge, 1993), pp. 196-211.

39. J. Jorge Klor de Alva, "Telling Hispanics Apart: Latino Sociocultural Diversity" in *The Hispanic Experience in the United States,* ed., Edna Acosta-Belen and Barbara R. Sjostrom (New York: Praeger, 1988), p. 133.

40. Established scholarship largely assumes such a normative standard of understanding race relations in the United States. See for instance, Cornel West, *Race Matters* (New York: Beacon Press, 1993); Herbert Hill and James E. Jones, Jr., ed. *Race in America: The Struggle for Equality* (Madison, Wis.: University of Wisconsin Press, 1993).

41. Ines Pinto Alicea, "Smithsonian Reaches Out to Latinos," *Hispanic Outlook* 5 (7), December 1, 1994, p. 4.

42. Ibid.

43. Rebecca Morales and Frank Bonilla, eds. *Latinos in a Changing U.S. Economy* (Newbury Park, Calif.: Sage Publications, 1993), p. 14.

44. Ibid., p. 227.

45. Walt Whitman, "The Spanish Element in Our Nationality" in *The Works of Walt Whitman,* Vol. 2, ed., M. Crowley (New York: Funk & Wagnalls, 1948), pp. 402-3.

46. Sam Roberts, "Census Reveals a Surge in Hispanic Population," the *New York Times,* 9 October 1994, sec. 15.

47. Earl Shorris, *Latinos: A Biography of the People* (New York: W. W. Norton and Company, 1992), pp. 47-50.

48. Edna Acosta-Belen, "From Settlers to Newcomers: The Hispanic Legacy in the United States" in *The Hispanic Experience in the United States,* ed., Edna Acosta-Belen and Barbara R. Sjostrom (New York: Praeger, 1988), p. 100.

49. Ibid.
50. See especially Delia Poey and Virgil Suare, eds. *Iguana Dreams: New Latino Fiction* (New York: HarperCollins, 1992); and Harold Aguenbraum and Ilan Stavans, eds. *Growing Up Latino: Memoirs and Stories* (New York: Houghton Mifflin, 1993).
51. Acosta-Belen, "From Settlers to Newcomers: The Hispanic Legacy in the United States," p. 100.
52. By culturally established Americans, I mean Black and White members of U.S. society whose identity is culturally constituted by a biologically based biracial normative gaze that influences the reading of history, national identity, and social relations.
53. See especially Rodolfo Acuna, *Occupied America: A History of Chicanos* (New York: Harper & Row, 1988); Ronald Takaki, *A Different Mirror: A History of Multicultural America* (Boston: Little, Brown and Company 1993); and Herbert Hill, "Black Workers, Organized Labor, and Title VII of the 1964 Civil Rights Act: Legislative History and Litigation Record," *Race in America,* ed., Herbert Hill and James E. Jones, Jr., p. 341.
54. Lee Romney and Jeff Brazil, "Boy's Death Stirs Debate Over California's Immigration Initiative" *The Washington Post,* 25 November 1994, sec. A3.

Chapter Two

Jesus at
the Margins

The Children

sitting on the steps down
on Boynton Avenue hanging
out looking at what is left

of us—this block, it all comes
so unexpectedly. days made drunk by
gin and beer issuing forth in cloudy

nights where needles still enter
waiting veins to further hide the
pain—on the block. faces aging

before their time telling of days
of life in dying pointing the way
to a captivity exercised now

in junkie nods that pace
conversation—it all comes so
unexpectedly. children playing on

the streets evolving into wise
miserable junkie men and women
filled with maturing rage only

silenced by the world in its
places of "lock-up." yes, this
block—it all comes so unexpectedly.

Since the Enlightenment, Christian scholars have struggled to understand the historical Jesus by situating his life in contexts not probed by Christian orthodoxy. Theologians have concentrated their quest for understanding on Jesus' sociocultural world, his ethical teachings, the meaning of his death during the rule of the Roman procurator Pontius Pilate (A.D. 26–36), or in terms of the faith of the church.[1] As historical and critical methodologies of interpretation evolved, it became clear that the Gospels reflect not so much a strict history of Jesus of Nazareth than interpretations of his life and work.

As Western intellectuals struggled to grasp the identity of Jesus, they turned to the more than fifty different apocryphal Gospels that survived in mostly fragmented form or to extrabiblical sources such as those written by Suetonius, Pliny, Tacitus, and Josephus, as well as to the Talmud and the Koran.[2] Each of these documents made varying degrees of reference to Jesus and the early church in ways that helped to elucidate the New Testament's assorted interpretations of Jesus of Nazareth. Indeed, this quest for the historical Jesus reflected a struggle to see the Carpenter from Nazareth not strictly in terms of a confession of faith but as a foundation-shaking question. Can this be one identifiable locus where the concerns of all Christians converge?

Christians largely relate to Jesus' identity in terms of its salvific value, which they sum up with the phrase, "Jesus saves." For many who seek a more meaningful way to live in a world that seems to be governed by overpowering systems of meaninglessness and injustice, Jesus is an answer. Yet, Christians everywhere are seeking to understand Jesus in the world in new ways. Jesus of Nazareth is now less likely to be placed above history and culture. Christians are insisting that Jesus be found at the center of their social reality. In the barrio, Latinos know Jesus as a foundation-shaking question that confronts the church. Racially scorned and socially invisible Latinos are revealing anew the empowering Spirit of God questioning human designs on life.

From the barrio, Latinos challenge mainline Christianity's ways of interpreting Jesus of Nazareth by relating his message to the world of overlooked people. In Latino worlds of concrete misery resulting from economic and political injustice, the questions that are posed to faith require answers that inspire social behavior that changes real conditions of life. Hence, Latinos are talking about a Jesus who, as a poor person who knew concrete misery and hope in God, perceived and criticized the mainline religious tradition of his day. Latinos find in the various interpretations of Jesus located in the New Testament a prophet who was critical of the way mainline religion backed social structures and rules that worked against creating a sense of real human solidarity.

Jesus, whose body is broken each day by the woeful social reality known to Latinos, asks through the experience of the barrio poor, "Who do you say that I am?" (see Mark 8:27-30; Matt. 16:13-20; Luke 9:18-21). That question is always answered in the context of a people's cultural history where the boundaries of human experience are defined. Customarily, the church has answered that Jesus is the Savior, the Son of God, a champion of nonviolence, the Lamb of God, brother, prophet, liberator, political revolutionary, Black Messiah, superstar, teacher, mystic Christ, Sophia, Prince of Peace, Consoler, unemployed laborer, an indigent, or social martyr.[3] Church tradition supports these responses.

Nevertheless, new ways of understanding Jesus can be discovered by those members of American society who walk the road to Emmaus that leads to solidarity with the racially oppressed and socially forgotten people of the barrio. The Holy Spirit invites the mainline church to confess that God is present in the Latino poor of the barrio. These children of God remind the larger society that all is not well in America. Their conditions of existence challenge those values too often promoted by mainline churches that give support to a socially indifferent status quo. Barrio Latinos who live in a permanent state of social and economic crisis bear witness to the One Crucified by ruling authorities and human villainy. This Jesus saves people from unjust suffering.

Poor Latino men, women, and children are reshaping the meaning of the words, "I will take you as my people, and I will be your God" (Exod. 6:7; see Jer. 7:23). Faith, seen in the perspective of the barrio, enables the mainline church to reclaim its identity in the God of lowly people. What is quite certain is that the God of the lowly, who favors those who suffer unjustly, liberates Latinos and all humanity from their despair and hopelessness. The biblical God of humble people saves the powerless for a new life that makes history. It is this God of whom the Bible speaks when it reports in Exodus of God acting in the world of Hebrew slaves who were dehumanized and excluded in Egypt from beneficial roles in social, political, cultural, and economic life.

The God of the lowly sides with an enslaved people who were subjected by a powerful empire to violent conditions of life. The power of Pharaoh, evident in the institution of slavery and the wretched basis of life it fostered, was vanquished by this loving God who hears, above all other voices, the cry of hurt people. This God of the lowly freed Hebrew slaves for a new life defined by equality in social relations. The witness of Scriptures never fails to report the varieties of ways that the God who knew the deep suffering of enslaved Hebrews in Egypt enters history identified with humble people. The God of the lowly is manifested in the mother of Jesus. Through Mary of Nazareth, God addresses all people from the position of lowliness and womanhood.

In the barrio Mary is an important symbol of faith, struggle, and future hope. What does she tell us about the God of the lowly or poor? Does the presence of this poor teen-mother from an insignificant part of the Jewish world proclaim God's unfolding dialogue with us? Clearly, Mary is a lowly woman of no social importance who listens closely to God's Word. Mary shows a spirit of trust and faith in God while dealing with the hard questions and struggles of life. She was always open and vulnerable to the unlimited and unpredictable nearness of the God of the lowly to those most in need. Like so many poor everywhere, Mary was humiliated by the status quo. Yet, she always remembered to express faith as a deep commitment to God and God's utter solidarity with the poor.

Mary of Nazareth speaks to us of a God who elevates women and the lowly in their society. Although rejected by persons adhering to patriarchal, cultural, and religious norms, Mary reveals the logic of the world turned on its head. This woman from a region of the world that is culturally lacking, a worthless barrio, is "blessed . . . among women" (Luke 1:42). Her life was unexpectedly changed by the God who favors those counted as nobody in the world. As a daughter of an oppressed and dominated people, the Magnificat attributed to her lips expresses how God remains faithful to the powerless. Like so many Latinas in the barrio, Mary confesses a God who has "looked with favor on the lowliness of his servant" (Luke 1:48). That term "lowliness" signifies affliction and oppression. That status concerns God.

From the humble setting of her barrio, Mary celebrates with the confidence of a prophet the reality of a God who scatters the proud in the imagination of their hearts, puts down the mighty from their thrones, exalts the oppressed poor, fills those who are hungry with good things, and sends the rich away with nothing. Wisdom comes from the experience of the lowly who see the face of God in their communities. The lowly know that God's ways are not the ways of human beings. The God of the lowly revealed by Mary disperses the arrogant who intend to humiliate and oppress the poor. God, who is powerful and merciful, is on the barrio side of town. God upsets powerful people who use their position to oppress those they consider worthy of all manner of abuse.

From Jesus' conception to the day she stood with the apostles when the Holy Spirit appeared in the form of fiery tongues to fill them (Acts 1:12-14; 2:1-4), Mary remained faithful to the God of the lowly. Mary backed God's plan for humanity that unfolded in her Son. She accompanied Jesus to the cross and played out her role in the process of building a new history. Like so many poor mothers, Mary suffered when her Son was arrested, beaten, tortured, and put to death by trusted authority figures. Yet, she knew in her heart (Luke 2:51) that Jesus had good news of a time when all people would have equal rights in a renewed social order. Because Mary revealed in prophetic words that God prefers the lowly and abused, she was nothing but a clear threat to the status quo.

In Mary's son, Jesus, the God of the lowly is further revealed in an unexpected place. In Jesus, the time of fulfillment appears in an existential context of utter marginality. Jesus was born in a stable among animals. The place stank. His birth was witnessed by lowly shepherds. Jesus was not an only child. He had four brothers and an unknown number of sisters whose names are not given in the Scriptures. Moreover, Jesus grew up in Nazareth, a town that stood some four miles from the more cosmopolitan city of Sepphoris, which had been destroyed by Roman soldiers while putting down a Jewish rebellion. Certainly, raised in Jewish tradition, Jesus likely learned to read and write by studying the Torah.

Because Jesus was a woodworker or Tekton, some might be inclined to believe that he was quite well-off; however, that form of labor placed Jesus among the marginalized classes of his day.[4] Already by the age of twelve, Jesus understood his identity in relation to God, which he tells his parents (Luke 2:43, 49). As an adult, Jesus preferred the company of people of humble social standing. Jesus was also not formally trained in theology and showed his concern primarily for the lowly people of the land who were rejected by dominant society. Jesus extended blessings to those who were rejected by official society. Having given this brief sketch, what can we find said of him in the tradition to answer the question, "Who do you say that I am?"

Prophet from the Lowly Side of Town

In Jesus of Nazareth the God who opposes the hateful purposes of human beings took the form of the lowly and despised poor. The reality of God gets enfleshed in a poor Jewish family far from the centers of power. That Jesus was reared in a lowly family shows God's special option for the poor and powerless. Interestingly, Pauline scholars largely agree that Paul did not focus on details of Jesus' life; yet, Paul recalls Jesus' humble origins when he writes that "our Lord Jesus Christ . . . became poor, so that by his poverty [we] might become rich" (2 Cor. 8:9). Born in the stench of a stable, Jesus revealed the God of the lowly who favors the poor and promises to create a new world for all human beings (Luke 4:18-20).

God favors social outcasts and poor people. The social geography of revelation points to God engaging human beings through the lowly who live at the margins of society. What are we to think of Jesus who came from a marginal region of the established Palestinian Jewish world?[5] Nathanael could not believe that "Jesus the Son of Joseph" is the one of "whom Moses in the law and also the prophets wrote" (John 1:45). Even Pharisees imparted to Nicodemus their rejection of the idea of a prophet coming from Galilee (John 7:52).[6] Many mainline Christians today have forgotten the prophetic identity of Jesus. Yet, Jesus who says "follow me" (Mark 1:17) is truly remembered as "the prophet who is to come into the world" (John 6:14; see also 4:19; 7:40; 9:17).

Jesus of Nazareth is seen as a prophet anointed by God to announce the inbreaking of the reign of God.[7] The unknown Nazarene prophet, who conducted most of his ministry in Galilee at a time when prophecy had declined in Israel, said, "The time is fulfilled, and the kingdom of God has come near" (Mark 1:14). Established culture may have rejected Jesus, but the people did not refrain from considering him in the prophetic line (Matt. 16:14; Mark 8:28; Luke 9:19). Indeed, the mostly lowly and marginal people who witnessed Jesus performing miracles were certain that a prophet was among them. After Jesus healed the widow's son in the city of Nain the people easily declared, "A great prophet has risen among us!" (Luke 7:16).[8]

That Jesus is thought of as a prophet is further evidenced in the account of the healing of the blind man of Bethsaida (Mark 8:22-27). Jesus heard the cry of a blind man whose sight he restored. Healing brought the gift of new life. Such moments in Jesus' healing ministry caused people to think of him as John the Baptist, Elijah, Jeremiah, or some other important Jewish prophet (Matt. 16:13-16; Mark 8:1-26; Luke 9:18-20). Educated Jews like Josephus and the rabbis looked down upon these prophecy beliefs held by the people that focused attention on miracle working.[9] Finally, the scribes and chief priests did not quickly arrest Jesus because they feared popular revolt from those tied to their prophet (Matt. 21:46; Mark 12:12; Luke 20:19).

In Luke, Jesus' prophetic status is established when he reads from a text in Isaiah to a mainline congregation (Isa. 61:1-2; 58:6) to disclose his mission plan for all humanity, and especially the poor. In public, Jesus reveals himself as the voice of the lowly and wretched who need liberation from the structures that exclude, exploit, and oppress them. As a prophet who comes from the ranks of the marginalized, Jesus' message subverts the class interests of the powerful. Thus, Luke proclaims the purpose of Jesus' ministry is to end poverty, unjust imprisonment, ignorance, and oppression (Luke 4:18-19). These situations are reflected in social structures that bring suffering and death to lowly people. Of course, after rejection by kinsfolk Jesus says, "No prophet is accepted in the prophet's hometown" (Luke 4:24-27; see also Mark 6:4).

What can we say about the Galilean prophet's home territory? Galilee was mostly poor, enclosed by Hellenistic cities, and cut off from the centers of economic, political, cultural, and social power in the South.[10] Jesus' world was also inhabited by Gentiles and Jews not unaccustomed to the process of racial and cross-cultural union.[11] Galilee was considered racially impure and culturally inferior, thus it was disapprovingly viewed by most of the more religiously and ethnically correct people to the south. Jesus' own genealogy makes him a cultural outsider. Jesus is related to a pagan, slaves, a lowly shepherd, a carpenter, a foreigner, prostitutes, and an adulteress (Matt. 1:1-16; Luke 1:26-27).[12] Thus, Jesus is both a rejected prophet and a nobody.

Jesus, who is among the world's nobodies, conducts a public ministry based on a theology that mainline religious officials reject. Jesus' rendition of the religious heritage of Israel quite clearly caused leaders to oppose him.[13] They rejected the idea of a layperson teaching with an authority unlike that of the correct leaders of established Judaism (Matt. 7:28-29). Jesus derived his authority to make all outsiders prevalent insiders from the Holy Spirit (Mark 1:10-11; Luke 4:18-19). In fact, Jesus taught about a new relationship between God and human beings, he healed the sick, forgave sins, and supplied new life to the dead. Mainline religious leaders still preferred to attribute Jesus' independent authority to Satan or Beelzebul, not God (Matt. 9:33-34; Luke 11:15).

His independent authority was reflected in his attitude toward women. For instance, Jesus refused to make objects of women by understanding them in terms of inferiority and their sex identity. He negated the idea common in his time that women were unclean. Jesus was no friend of the prevailing culture that misconstrued the personhood of women; meanwhile, he scandalized peers and followers by his behavior toward women. As we can see, the scripture reports that Jesus had women among his followers and disciples:

> Soon afterwards he went on through cities and villages, proclaiming and bringing the good news of the kingdom of God. The twelve were with him, as well as some women who had been cured of evil spirits and infirmities: Mary, called Magdalene, from whom seven demons had gone out, and Joanna, the wife of Herod's steward Chuza, and Susanna, and many others, who provided for them out of their resources. (Luke 8:1-3; 23:49)

The place held by women in Jesus' community signified that women were truly affirmed.[14]

Jesus broke social rules by speaking in public with Jewish women and those discounted as heretics. He conversed with a Samaritan woman despite the outrage of close followers. That Samaritan woman who debated with Jesus became nothing less than a source of evangelization to her people. She symbolized a rebuttal of the system of male authority that cast women in a subordinate and oppressive role in society.[15] Jesus was also seen breaking the religious and cultural standards of his day by taking the side of an adulterous woman:

> Early in the morning he came again to the temple. All the people came to him and he sat down and began to teach them. The scribes and the Pharisees brought a woman who had been caught in adultery; and making her stand before all of them, they said to him, "Teacher, this woman was caught in the very act of committing adultery. Now in the law Moses commanded us to stone such women. Now what do you say?" (John 8:2-5)

Jesus opposed the law that demanded the woman's life, given that it was not based on the equality of persons.

Jesus received the adulterous woman as a full human being. He defied the male double standard that demanded capital punishment for her, although allowing an adulterous man to face a lesser charge. Hence, he says "Let anyone among you who is without sin be the first to throw a stone at her" (John 8:7). The mainline religious leaders actually showed no real concern for the situation of the adulterous woman or even the meaning of the law. Both the law and the adulterous woman were, for them, instruments with which to oppose the authority of Jesus and establish a basis for his annihilation. Nonetheless, Jesus stunned the public by offering forgiveness, demanding change, and rejecting a moral law that unjustly discriminated against women.[16]

By all counts, the good news of Jesus subverts the rules of exclusion demanded by the mainline piety of his day. Jesus was critical of a mainline religious tradition whose rules of piety defined who was an insider (see especially Mark). For Jesus, all people are children of God; thus, religious codes that alienate people from God and one another need breaking (Mark 7:9; Matt. 15:1-9). In light of his understanding of God's will for humanity, Jesus openly embraces social outcasts, rejects laws of exclusion, and practices an inclusivity that brings a genuine experience of God. Still, the religious leaders rejected Jesus who gladly announced a new way of life together in love, unity, and equality (Mark 1:1; 15:39).

Interestingly, Mark presents the scribes, Pharisees, Herodians, chief priests, elders, and Sadducees as a united front against Jesus.[17] Even an unlikely coalition forms between the Pharisees and Herodians who plan to kill Jesus (Mark 3:6). Pious Jews did often wonder where a carpenter born to a poor woman acquired his unique understanding on matters related to their mainline religion (Mark 6:1-6; Matt. 13:53-58). Despite opposition, Jesus broke the religiously sanctioned norms of the mainline religion of his people that largely generated situations of social alienation.[18] We can tell that Jesus' healing ministry, directed mostly to social outcasts, confronted the purity, debt, and holiness codes upheld by mainline religious officials.[19]

For instance, when Jesus healed a leper he broke the purity regulations (Lev. 13:2–14:57) that included separating the ill from the rest of the community, and ritual cleansing by a priest.[20] Religious leaders rejected the idea of Jesus venturing to defy the Torah by touching and healing a leper (Mark 1:40-45). Jesus also broke the debt code when he cured a paralytic in Capernaum. Illness was mostly considered a punishment or a consequence of sin; however, Jesus defied the debt code that would have attributed the paralytic's condition to either individual or inherited sin. Jesus knew that the sick and physically impaired of Palestinian society were condemned by law to be non-persons in the community and that they faced certain poverty.

Although no more than a lay teacher of religion, Jesus fully forgave the paralytic and commanded him to rise from his bed of poverty and go home (Mark 2:11). The scribes, who controlled access to forgiveness because of their authority to interpret the law and indebtedness, were furious.[21] Finally, Jesus confronted the established holiness code associated with keeping the sabbath.[22] In Mark 3:1-6, Jesus met in the synagogue a man with a withered hand whose condition was not existentially recognized by the mainline religious officials. The Pharisees failed to see the man with the withered hand as a child of God who was in desperate need of healing; instead, the man with the withered hand was merely an object of theological debate.

The law-abiding Pharisees preferred to watch Jesus, waiting to accuse him of breaking the law. Healing on the sabbath, which they considered a generally prohibited form of work, was, after all, a capital offense! Jesus, who heals the man with the withered hand on the sabbath, shows that God's merciful action works against the traditional rules. A loving God does not marginalize those in need. God is a God of life, not rules. Yet, on that Sabbath, stubborn religious leaders planned evil (Mark 3:6). Jesus violated the purity code as well when he healed the woman who suffered a flow of blood for twelve years, causing her to exist in a state of ritual death by virtue of being considered impure and an outcast.

The cultural and religious standards required that Jesus stay away from the sick. They were considered dirty. But God-in-Jesus showed favor and restored that long-suffering and lowly woman to wholeness.

Jesus awakened in the afflicted woman the power of her own faith in God to heal. He says, "Daughter, your faith has made you well; go in peace" (Luke 8:48). Jesus healed the woman in public and restored her to life in the view of society. What became evident to those who followed Jesus[23] is that he was not like the learned theologians of mainline religion with whom he came into conflict.[24] The lowly people of the barrios of Galilee who witnessed these healing miracles believed in Jesus. Only Jesus refused to make their suffering an abstract affair.

Mainline religious officials, unconvinced of the authority of Jesus, wanted proof. They even demanded a sign from heaven (Mark 8:11). Jesus delivered a different sign. He confronted the economic interests of the priestly aristocracy and the ruling classes who together extracted wealth from the poor. Their commercial system turned the Temple into a "den of robbers" (Mark 11:17). Jesus' protest inflamed the chief priests and scribes of the law (Mark 11:18). These established religious leaders who operated out of the wisdom of materialism, militarism, and legalism radically opposed Jesus. They asked him, "By what authority are you doing these things?" (Mark 11:27). After the cleansing of the Temple, Jesus fatally confronted the mainline religious establishment (Mark 11:15–16:8).

What do we learn from Jesus' conflict with the mainline religious tradition? What does his identity in the lowly and the Galilean periphery say to us? Jesus revealed a God that is neither remote, limited to the views of religious officials, nor captive of the Torah as interpreted by them. Jesus broke the law to reveal how God's love reinstated the personhood of the lowly and socially outcast. Jesus revealed a God who is with us and is opposed to the social, economic, and political walls erected with the help of religion. For Jesus, God is not found in external institutions like the law or the Temple; instead, God approaches humanity enfleshed in the sick and socially excluded who seek hope and a new life.

Barrio Christianity Proclaims Good News

Who is Jesus in mainline Christianity? In one mainline religious view, Jesus is depicted as the suffering Christ who is accessible to people whose own suffering requires comforting (Matt. 11:28-30). Those who see the suffering Christ look to him to learn how to survive in bad situations; yet, Jesus does not move persons to examine the social construction of their pain. Because this view of Jesus drives faith inward, and produces a sense of resignation before social reality, the suggestion that the world cannot be radically transformed obtains religious proof. For countless mainline Christians undergoing assorted and trying life situations, a suffering Christ provides an answer to hard times. Nonetheless, Jesus requires individuals to develop a more critical understanding of the basis of their personal and social aches.

An ahistorical image of the suffering Jesus negates the gospel's unapologetic challenge to all forms of social life that cause human affliction. A Jesus who only provides consolation for persons crushed by a historical reality capable and deserving of change merits no following from God's people. Jesus' suffering directs us to question the meaning of the histories of women, the poor, and all people in desperate need. A Jesus who reveals that God is with the lowly utters good news of change to hurting people. What is certain is that those who find solace in the image of a suffering Jesus are summoned to discover Christ's presence in the anguish of the poor and oppressed. This means mainline churches are to heal, teach, and attend to people's needs.

A second view of Jesus found in mainline churches presents Jesus as the glorified Christ who overcomes death and the sins of the world (John 17:4-5). This exalted Christ enchants a following of persons who hope to rise above the disorder of everyday life. A glorified Christ appeals to individuals who want to understand themselves in the context of salvation beyond history. In Jesus, they find the one who is "able for all time to save those who approach God . . . since he always lives to make intercession for them" (Heb. 7:25). This Christology interprets the gospel as a promise of personal salvation apart from social, economic, political, and institutional renewal. Proponents of this viewpoint are least likely to relate God's Word to saving daily action.

Neither an ahistorical reading of the experience of suffering nor the single focus on personal salvation as flight from the world bears the good news promised by Jesus the prophet from Nazareth. The poor, racially despised groups, women discriminated against, and social outcasts require a new and more hopeful reading of Jesus' ministry. The leper who was cleansed, the man with the withered hand who was cured, and the woman who recovered from years of bleeding show us Jesus' power to bring change in history. Mainline churches that confess Christ glorified must recognize that he brought change to the oppressed and rejected (Heb. 4:15–5:10). Indeed, Christ suffered death on the cross to change human history (Phil. 2:6-8).

Too many mainline churches have reduced the practice of ministry to mere Sabbath observance. Many mainline Christians have forgotten that Jesus said "the sabbath was made for humankind, and not humankind for the sabbath" (Mark 2:27). That Jesus healed on the Sabbath (see Mark 2:1-5) confirms Jesus' understanding that the Sabbath for mainline religious communities ought to reveal God as One-for-Others in concrete history. Mainline Christians must acknowledge that their churches form part of God's mission action that makes a new way of life available to all human beings. Indeed, the glorified Christ sent the Holy Spirit to build a church able to alter unjust economic systems and patterns of social exclusion (1 Cor. 1:27-28; Acts 2:42-47; 4:32–5:11).

The Spirit is now enabling mainline Christians to see the Jesus who is at the center of a new barrio Christianity. Here we find a hard-hitting Jesus who promises life in abundance and does not avoid situations of social conflict (Matt. 10:34-37; Mark 10:29-31; Luke 12:52-53). "Do not think that I have come to bring peace to the earth; I have not come to bring peace, but a sword" (Matt. 10:34). This Jesus calls disciples to vacate the established world that displays so little humanity and stand in solidarity with all people in justice and love. This Jesus weeps and labors with the poor who are nobody in society. The hard-hitting Jesus roots ecclesial identity in the world of social outcasts whose cries drown out all others. This Jesus invites outcasts to community in God. This Jesus says stay close to those who suffer oppression.

The hard-hitting Jesus who declares good news to all humanity stands with the poor, denounces the accumulation of wealth, praises individuals who give up their love of money, rejects oppressive behavior, demands that service and humility define community, and makes opposition to social injustice essential. The hard-hitting Jesus tells global peasants and those at the margins of the urban world that their poverty implicates the rich (Luke 6:24; 12:13-21), religious authorities (Luke 11:39-44; 46-54; Mark 11:15-39), and powerful officials (Mark 10:42). The living conditions of the poor evidence the negation of life by these privileged classes who unfold oppressive practices.[25]

The hard-hitting Jesus reveals a God who is not separate from the religious, economic, and political institutions that conduct the affairs of history. This Jesus tells us God has authority over these cultural structures. Because the gospel addresses these areas and disciples are sent to engage them, followers will experience conflict in history (Luke 21:12-13; 22:36; Mark 13:9). The hard-hitting Jesus warns followers that for promoting the good news of a just society

> they will arrest you and persecute you; they will hand you over to syn-agogues and prisons, and you will be brought before kings and governors because of my name. This will give you an opportunity to testify. (Luke 21:12-13)

Nonetheless, the hard-hitting Jesus demands that one take a firm stand before the powerful.

The hard-hitting Jesus understood the oppressive mechanisms of the rich in light of the hope of the lowly for a genuinely humanizing society (Matt. 6:24; Luke 6:24). He radically affirmed the poor in the ultimate soil of human life: the God who is Father and Mother of all Creation. It is the hard-hitting Jesus who makes Christians "rich out of his poverty" (see 2 Cor. 8:9). This prophet from Nazareth seeks to shape the church into a collective gospel force to demand better healthcare, housing, education, economic equality, and political voice for spurned human beings. The reign of God that the hard-hitting Jesus preached is present where situations of social injustice, class inequality, and human suffering are altered by church efforts (Luke 1:46-55).

A Parable: The Rich Man and Lazarus

A parable that reflects barrio Christianity's hard-hitting Jesus is the story of the rich man and Lazarus (Luke 16:19-31). This story tells of the rich whose material conditions of life can serve the poor. This parable focuses attention on the reversal of fortune in the afterlife. The social reality described is analogous to the relations between poor communities and affluent ones. In the parable, the reality of the poor is imaged by the man named Lazarus who is a beggar suffering from a skin disease. Lazarus does not have fine linen or feast sumptuously every day. Lazarus waits to eat the crumbs that fall from the wealthy man's table. He lacks.

In the story, God takes the side of Lazarus who is not wealthy and is a social nobody. This is made plain by the fact that in the story the rich man is nameless.[26] Most likely, the name of the rich man was known by most of the members of his society. That is easy to imagine. Many of us today find it easy to write a list of the rich and important families of American society. What is harder to do is learn the names of homeless individuals living on city streets in places all over America. Popular journals keep people informed about the lives of the rich and famous; however, the names of families forced by economic structures and discriminatory practices to live on the sub-poverty wages of welfare hardly make the news and almost always remain unspoken. Yet, God names the nameless!

The poor man Lazarus walks on the streets and rural roads of many communities across the country. Because God names the anonymous of history, the hard-hitting Jesus asks us to consider that Lazarus speaks to our affluent society now by way of the crucified people living in the barrio. Those who live at the margins of society know God favors them. God calls by name those persons who exist, despised and rendered invisible by those who control wealth, power, and dominant cultural viewpoints. God tells us to find God in the world of the utterly rejected. One Salvadoran friend said of this God, present in rejected and suffering humanity:

> When reading the gospel one feels that it was written directly for people like me who have suffered. Suffering happens to us, but God does not will human suffering. Those who suffer persecution, torture, murder, massacre, displacement, hunger, and refugee life are the Christ of our time. You see Christ in suffering people. I must try to

do what Christ did, struggle for what Christ struggled for, and live as Christ lived. Jesus lived and died for the poor. We must do the same thing.

The hard-hitting Jesus teaches that the God who favors Lazarus and persons who suffer unjustly like him passes judgment on those who too easily turn their backs. God particularly notices people who make their home in the inner city and country shacks, are utterly forgotten by the powerful, and are sinfully sacrificed each day to sudden or gradual unnatural death. Lazarus enjoys the place of honor in God's reign. In contrast, the nameless rich man who ignored God's command to do justice to the poor is severely judged. The rich man is delivered to a state of permanent suffering in the flames of hades for not upholding the covenant—God's will.[27] The rich man's neglect of the needs of the poor condemned him to separation from God who gives life.

The hard-hitting Jesus was not expounding a teaching on the life beyond death. That he was not recommending that the poor learn to be resigned to their life conditions is no less obvious. Jesus explicitly alludes to a form of society that shuts out God's Word and overvalues the personal security believed found in concentrated wealth. In short, the parable addresses current life by issuing a singular word of warning to structures of wealth that cost the life of those it excludes.[28] The hard-hitting Jesus warns those who enjoyed status and rank in their society about such idolatry. If the rich man's five brothers do not honor the glory of God that is the living poor person, they too will experience the meaning of God's endless absence.

In the story, the hard-hitting Jesus reminds those who believe they can serve money that the existential situation of Lazarus presupposes the reality of God. In other words, God is first revealed in the world of the lowly and oppressed. Money and power are idols when they replace trust in the Lord who speaks to all humanity from the painful depths of the marginalized. No amount of wealth will give human beings access to God; instead, by serving God in the concrete situations of the needy, one is opened to the gift of divine union. Lazarus reveals God as the strength that is present in the weakness of those who exist in life-denying conditions. Jesus tells us in this story that the suffering of the poor is overcome when people truly care enough to meet the poor's needs.

The rich man's sin consisted of neglect for a poor person whose suffering could be corrected by an act of love. The practice of indifference finally sanctioned and perpetuated Lazarus's wretched conditions of life. Most often, the privileged classes in society are agents of a similar destructive pattern that defines their relationship to the poor and unimportant. Jesus here teaches that wealth is not to be selfishly accumulated and used; instead, affluence is to be distributed across society in the function of serving the needs of all—especially the poor Lazaruses of our time!

The hard-hitting Jesus who entered society smelling of the stable tells us to find our true identity in Lazarus's loathsome world. In that world, God makes a home among poor men, women, and children who are homeless on city streets each day. The hard-hitting Jesus asks mainline Christians who are concerned with responding to the Lazaruses of their society, "What does it mean to have thirty-six million people in this country alone living at or below the official poverty standard each year? Why does America have more poor people than the total combined populations of the forty largest American cities, double the combined populations of the seven nations of Central America, or more than the total number of seconds in a year?"[29]

Marginalized people, such as the thirty-six million poor in the United States, need to be seen as the living image of our Crucified God who demands the work of justice from the church. Lazarus is at the door of mainline churches in these poor who are living on the edge of society. Undoubtedly, profound honesty about social reality will lead members of mainline churches to encounter the hard-hitting Jesus who takes the form of the poor, "those other people." Once mainline churches agree to discover their life in the barrios that have been rejected by mainstream society, new questions and directions for faith will be found. Mainline churches must bear witness to the God who brings life out of death and hope out of despair in the context of people's daily struggle in the world.

The hard-hitting Jesus says Christians cannot remain passive as physical and spiritual death walks through so many communities claiming the lives of forgotten people. The Lazaruses of our time expect mainline churches to offer the hope and organization for social change promised by the message of Jesus. Mainline churches need to break the cultural rules that keep people from seeing the suffering at the bottom of society. The hard-hitting Jesus asks us to build a church that is conscious of a creation that groans to be free from the bondage of social and physical disintegration (Rom. 8:22). Through Christian action, others will learn that the light of Christ cannot be engulfed by the turmoil and dusk of the world. This is the way of political holiness.[30]

Notes

1. John H. Hayes, *Son of God to Super Star: Twentieth-Century Interpretations of Jesus* (Nashville: Abingdon Press, 1976), pp. 13-14.
2. Ibid., pp. 32-33.
3. See C. S. Song, *Jesus: The Crucified People* (New York: Crossroad, 1990); and John H. Hayes, *Son of God to Super Star: Twentieth-Century Interpretations of Jesus* (Nashville: Abingdon Press, 1976).
4. Marcus J. Borg, *Meeting Jesus Again for the First Time* (New York: HarperCollins, 1995), p. 26.
5. See Virgilio Elizondo, *Galilean Journey: The Mexican American Promise* (Maryknoll, N.Y.: Orbis Books, 1983); and Orlando E. Costas, Liberating News: A Theology of Contextual Evangelization (New York: Eerdmans, 1989).
6. Virgilio Elizondo, the Mexican American theologian and priest, has produced a theology of *mestizaje* that stations God's revelation in the precise reality of racial and cultural admixture. Mestizaje is foundational for the rejection of Galilee by Southern Jews who believed themselves to be the guardians of pure religious and cultural life. Orlando E. Costas views Galilee as the periphery of society that becomes an instrument of evangelization. Hence, Galilee defines the context, character, and purpose of the church's evangelistic mission. Building on their work, I emphasize the prophetic stance of Jesus who comes from a Galilean barrio.
7. Ched Meyers, *Binding the Strong Man: A Political Reading of Mark's Story of Jesus* (Maryknoll, N.Y.: Orbis Books, 1994), pp. 123-24.
8. The story of the widow's son parallels accounts of the "wonder-work" of two intertestamental Judaism biblical characters known as Elijah and Elisha. Luke's account of the raising of the widow's son in Nain is clearly patterned after the

story of Elijah found in 1 Kings 17:9-10, 17-24. In 1 Kings, at Zarephath, located near Sidon, Elijah raised a widow's son; meanwhile, Elisha is reported to have performed such a miracle at Shunem (2 Kings 4:32-37). The story of Jesus feeding a crowd (Matt. 14:13-21; Mark 6:30-43; Luke 9:10-17) is akin to Elisha's feeding of a hundred men (2 Kings 4:43-44). Evidently, the plain reliance on the book of Kings and the figures of Elijah and Elisha partly indicate that the Synoptics locate Jesus in a prophetic context.

9. Geza Vermes, *Jesus the Jew* (London: Collins, 1973), p. 93.

10. Meyers, *Binding the Strong Man*, p. 128.

11. Costas, *Liberating News: A Theology of Contextual Evangelization*, p. 51; and Elizondo, *Galilean Journey*, p. 51.

12. Elizondo, *Galilean Journey*, p. 55; and Meyers, *Binding the Strong Man*, p. 128.

13. R. David Kaylor, *Jesus the Prophet: His Vision of the Kingdom On Earth* (Louisville: Westminster/John Knox Press, 1994).

14. Gustavo Gutierrez, *The God of Life* (Maryknoll, N.Y.: Orbis Books, 1991), p. 16.

15. Ibid., p. 168.

16. Ibid., p. 169.

17. Jack Dean Kingsbury, "The Religious Authorities in the Gospel of Mark," *New Testament Studies* 36 (1990): 42-65.

18. Meyers, *Binding the Strong Man*, p. 137.

19. At the beginning of Mark's Gospel five controversies are reported that reflect Jesus' tension with the mainline religious officials (2:1–3:6). For instance, Jesus heals a paralytic and scribes charge him with blasphemy (2:1-12)—the charge that condemns Jesus to death (14:64). He breaks the Pharisaic rules of table fellowship by eating with tax collectors and sinners and is questioned (2:15-17). His disciples do not fast like other religious people (2:18-22) and they work on the sabbath (2:23-28). He enters the sacred space of the synagogue and heals a man with a withered hand and publicly violates the sabbath law (3:1-5).

20. Meyers, *Binding the Strong Man*, p. 152.

21. Ibid., p. 155; also Kaylor, *Jesus the Prophet*, p. 186.

22. Meyers, *Binding the Strong Man*, p. 158.

23. The healing ministry of Jesus is a sign of his role as a prophet. It is attested by the synoptic Gospels. For instance, Jesus heals members of the crowd in Capernaum (Mark 1:32-34) and Galilee (Mark 3:7-12; 6:53-56). Jesus' healing ministry encompassed three cases of blindness (Mark 8:22-26; 10:46-52; Matt. 9:27-31) and two of leprosy (Mark 1:40-44; Luke 17:11-19). Jesus healed Simon's mother-in-law of fever (Mark 1:29-31); he healed the woman with a flow of blood (Mark 5:25-34), the man with the withered hand (Mark 3:1-5), deafness (Mark 7:31-37), paralysis (Mark 2:3-11; Matt. 8:5-13), and the lameness of a woman (Luke 13:10-13).

24. See Jack Dean Kingsbury, *Conflict & Mark: Jesus, Authorities, Disciples* (Minneapolis: Fortress, 1989).

25. Phillip Berryman, *The Religious Roots of Rebellion: Christians in Central American Revolutions* (Maryknoll, N.Y.: Orbis Books, 1986), p. 378.

26. See Joachim Jeremias, *The Parables of Jesus* (New York: Scribners, 1954), p. 183.

27. See Gutierrez, *The God of Life*, pp. 57-58.

28. See Jeremias, *The Parables of Jesus*, p. 186.

29. Joel A. Devine and James D. Wright, *The Greatest of Evils: Urban Poverty and the American Underclass* (Hawthorne, N.Y.: Aldine de Gruyter, 1993), pp. 29-30.

30. Church activism flows from following the hard-hitting Jesus whose consequence issues forth in genuine structural changes that concretely benefit those persons who are least among the more privileged members of society.

Chapter Three

The Cross

The Crucified

you never talk of the
barrio where
the words of the

poor cut away
the fat of a world
secure in wealth.

you never think
of the crucified
in the slums nailed

daily by bullets
to a wood that ejects
all hope tomorrow.

you were not there
to see the blood-stained
corner made by a four-

year-old girl who
received the bitter
end of a shoot-out

between fifteen-year-old
boys over the wrong
look on faces.

you refuse to walk
on the hard side of life
with a pity that plunges

your humanity into a
sea of rage of those whose
life unnaturally

finished. why do you wait to find
the Truth behind the walls of homes,
churches and in your head?

Don't you know Truth
waits for you in
the barrio in the

scarred flesh of Christ
in the poor?

Many Christians want to experience a new encounter with Jesus in their lives. Some are turning to Jesus of Nazareth and the witness of the church with deep questions about faith in the context of a troubled world. Christians and newcomers to the church are reexamining the history of Christianity for answers concerning the identity of Jesus. They are finding in the early church creeds a formulated understanding of Jesus' identity. For instance, after three hundred years of persecution and Constantine's adoption of Christianity, the Nicene Confession of 325 C.E. was formulated by the organized church. It reads, in part:

We believe in one God, the Father almighty, maker of all things visible and invisible;
And in one Lord Jesus Christ, the Son of God, begotten from the

Father, only-begotten, that is, from the substance of the Father, God from God, light from light, true God from true God, begotten not made, of one substance with the Father, through Whom all things came into being, things in heaven and things on earth, Who because of us [humans] and because of our salvation came down and became incarnate, becoming [human], suffered and rose again on the third day, ascended to the heavens, and will come to judge the living and the dead;

And in the Holy Spirit.[1]

Global Christianity treats these words as a basic confession of faith. Still, the Nicene Confession answers only some of the questions about Jesus.

The Apostles' Creed, which was formulated much later, today continues to be given a great deal of importance in Christian services of worship. I have been in Pentecostal storefront churches in the barrio and heard repeated the words of this creed in charismatic liturgy. The Apostles' Creed confesses Jesus is God, and adds historical items concerning Jesus' birth, life, and death as a human being:

And in Jesus Christ his only Son our Lord:
who was conceived by the Holy Spirit,
   born of the Virgin Mary,
   suffered under Pontius Pilate,
   was crucified, dead, and buried;
the third day he rose from the dead;
he ascended into heaven,
and sitteth at the right hand of God the Father Almighty; from thence he shall come to judge the quick and the dead.[2]

Still, this creed says nothing about Jesus' poverty and liberating work. Latinos now reveal new ways to understand the identity of Jesus as the Crucified God.

Latinos understand the central symbol of Christianity to be the cross. Even now, in barrios across the nation, Latinos perform the stations of the cross to contemporize and reflect on the meaning of the suffering and death of Jesus. The cross is a basic symbol that provides a semantic structure to Christian identity. Surely, most

Christians would agree that God addresses humanity through the human suffering and degradation of Christ on the cross; however, too many have forgotten that the cross points to the experience of rejection. Jesus on the cross died as one who was rejected by the law, society, and religion. All of society's rejects and outcasts look to the cross that condemns their status as nobodies and empowers them to be fully human in Jesus.

Latinos know that Jesus' suffering and death on the cross speaks directly to the world of the barrio where oppressed conditions of life demoralize the people's humanity. Jesus on the cross was disfigured by powerful social leaders and their political and religious institutions. Jesus' humanity, crushed on the cross, is a symbol of the experience of Latino existence that motivates radical opposition to life-denying situations. In the barrio, Latinos understand the cross was a consequence of Jesus' preaching of inclusivity, his freedom from boundary-making laws, and his table fellowship with people rejected by "civil" society. The hard-hitting prophet from Nazareth confronted reality from the position of the least in the community.

Christians who take the meaning of the cross for granted need to realize that the cross images forsakenness and disgrace. For instance, in the religion of ancient Israel, death on a tree signified exclusion from the established community. Death on a tree was interpreted in Israelite religion as God's curse and punishment for criminality (Deut. 21:23; Gal. 3:13). In ancient Roman culture, death on the cross was reserved for runaway slaves and those revolting against the Empire. Such a perverse symbol could hardly manifest the being of God. Yet, early Christians remained faithful to the God they believed was crucified in Christ, disavowing loyalty to the gods of the Roman state. Such loyalty won them the enmity of the Empire.

Surely, the cross signifies what many racially oppressed people like Latinos know from experience. First, the cross indicates the nearness of God to human pain. On the wood of the cross, God is present to human beings in their torment, sorrow, and hope for new life. On the cross, God is vulnerable and concretely present in all the inhumanity of history. Second, on the cross, unjust suffering becomes a part of God's self-identity and its existence in the world and the barrio is radically questioned. Third, the One who is nailed to the cross is a person of color who enfleshed the Word in the condition of social disadvantage. And fourth, the cross designates God's solidarity with the persecuted through the Son who was killed by people corrupted by power.

As mainline Christians struggle to understand their identity for the next century, they need to remember that the cross was a radically new religious understanding that in the early Christian world was thought a "stumbling block to Jews and foolishness to Gentiles" (1 Cor. 1:23). In other words, we must not forget that Christian faith originates outside the bounds of mainline religion and dominant culture where the reality of God is most radically introduced. The cross separates the church from the surrounding civilization by permanently criticizing the society-favoring tendency of mainline religion and the inherited interests of contemporary culture. Indeed, the cross frees human beings to confront the world with the truth of God.[3]

If the cross is going to be reclaimed as a symbol of Christian identity, it will be necessary to understand some aspects of the social world of Jesus' ministry. Contemporary Christians spend very little reflective time questioning the meaning of Jesus' death on the cross at the hands of both the Romans and a subdivision of mainline religious leaders. Clearly, as mainline churches have interpreted their mission outside of the arena of social history, it has become easier to find in Jesus' message only counsel for the soul and silence about politics, economics, culture, and social relationships. Let us now examine certain aspects of Jesus' social world to contextualize the meaning of the cross.

Aspects of Jesus' Social World

Since Jerusalem fell to the Babylonians in 587 B.C.E., Jewish society in Palestine came under the rule of Persia, Alexander the Great of Macedonia, Alexander's successors the Ptolemies of Egypt, and the

Seleucids of Syria.[4] By 63 B.C.E. when Rome asserted control over Palestine and the Near Eastern world, the Hellenistic Empire of the Seleucids was declining.[5] Rome dominated matters in Jewish society, abetted by the Herodian client kings and those among the Jewish elite who benefited economically and politically from foreign rule.[6] Evidently, in Jesus' day, imperial Rome and the subject status of Jewish society gave rise to a state of popular resistance and social conflict. Jesus was killed by the Romans by a method used on non-Romans judged outlaws by the state.[7]

Herod the Great ruled over Judea from c. 37 B.C.E. until his death in 4 B.C.E. Herod, a client king of Rome, served the interests of Octavian, who was bestowed by the Roman senate with the title of Augustus, the exalted one. His political position was dependent largely on actual social relations with Augustus and other privileged persons in the Roman state.[8] With the aid of Roman troops, Herod the Great seized Jerusalem and defended his regime through a merciless and oppressive domestic policy.[9] Although Herod the Great was "tolerant" of Judaism and identified himself as a Jew, his rule was hated by Jews because it resulted in an enormous tax burden, political and economic oppression, and the promotion of non-Jewish culture.[10]

For instance, heavy taxation was needed to finance the many building projects initiated by Herod. Among Herod's many building works were the rebuilding and expansion of the Temple in Jerusalem, a winter palace in Jericho, a magnificent palace in Jerusalem, an amphitheater, and temples erected in honor of the emperor in cities not populated with a Jewish majority—such as Samaria, Caesarea, and Antipatris.[11] Jews were offended when Herod affixed the golden eagle to the gate of the Temple. That symbol evidenced alien rule and economic hardship in Jewish society. Herod refused to take down the golden eagle. The scribes Judas and Matthias were killed after their followers cut it down.[12] Herod also clashed with some six thousand Pharisees who were fined after refusing to take an oath of loyalty to him and the emperor.[13] Because Herod the Great ennobled the Hellenization of Jewish culture, foreign rule, and engaged in economic and politically oppressive practices, his rule was hated by Jews;

yet during the 25 B.C.E. famine he used palace wealth to buy corn in Egypt to feed the hungry.

Illness claimed Herod the Great's life in 4 B.C.E. From his deathbed Herod named his son Archelaus to rule over Judea, Idumaea, and Samaria; meanwhile, Herod Antipas, named in honor of his grandfather Antipater of Edom, was named ruler of Galilee and Peraea and assumed the title of tetrarch.[14] Another brother, Philip, ruled in the north and east. After Herod's death, unrest erupted in response to the martyrdom of Judas and Matthias. Jews believed Archelaus would be responsive to their demands for tax restructuring, release of prisoners, removal of the high priest, and punishment for officials who killed the Jews who cut down the golden eagle;[15] yet, prior to departure for Rome for confirmation as Herod's successor, Archelaus used troops to put down the popular revolt.

Nevertheless, popular unrest persisted, commanding the response of Varus who was then governor of Syria. Three legions were marched to Judea to repress the social upheaval. Varus thought that order was restored when he departed for Antioch, leaving the procurator Sabinus behind at the head of a garrison. Hostilities erupted again because of Sabinus's persistent harassment of Jews and his apparent intention to capture the royal treasuries.[16] Jerusalem's population had swelled with mostly peasant pilgrims arriving for the Pentecost Festival as new clashes unfolded. The peasantry in the countryside of Galilee, Peraea, and Judea were also rebelling. Varus returned to Palestine and militarily put down the revolts. About two thousand of those who rebelled were crucified.[17]

Both John the Baptist and Jesus conducted their ministries in Galilee during the rule of Herod Antipas (c. 4 B.C.E.–A.D. 39). Herod Antipas not only ruled over socially unsettled Galilee, but he managed to stay in power without difficulty for some forty-three years.[18] That he was favored by the emperor Tiberius, after whom the city of Tiberias was named, partly assured the stability of his rule. Surely Herod Antipas's promotion of Hellenistic culture—seen especially in the transformation of the destroyed city of Sepphoris into a model cosmopolitan city—placed him in good standing with the Romans.[19] The scriptures record that Herod Antipas—who rejected a first wife in order to marry Herodias, the former wife of his brother Philip—had John the Baptist imprisoned and ordered his grisly murder.

Mostly, rural peasants continued to experience onerous economic conditions during the ruling of Herod Antipas. Although economic prosperity increased for port cities and the towns of the Transjordan that were relatively integrated into systems of trade and commerce, ordinary rural farmers remained at a disadvantage.[20] One consequence of the uneven development that worked to the advantage of the wealthy urban elite was rural land dispossession. Landholding peasants were forced to sell their plots for reasons such as illness, a bad growing season, or taxation.[21] As land was basically amassed by the Jerusalem leadership and turned into large estates, former landholding farmers would then be hired as day-workers (Matt. 20:1-15).[22]

In the agrarian world of Galilee, the large estate owners were typically members of the Jerusalem elite who often placed stewards in charge of their property (Luke 16:1-8). Moreover, tenant farming was not uncommon in the Galilean world where Jesus conducted most of his ministry. Tenant farmers surrendered between a half or a third of their harvest to the landowner and had to pay a produce tax and a toll tax to the state that covered cost of trade, commerce, and physical infrastructure.[23] That sharecroppers lived under difficult conditions and likely hoped to subvert the social relationship between the absentee landowners and themselves is arguably part of the larger context of the allegorical parable of the wicked tenants (Mark 12:1-11).[24]

In Galilean society, where farming was a basic mode of existence and a system of land dispossession prevailed, the jobless waited for work on a daily basis. Many of the impoverished became debtors who were forced to compensate creditors by offering their families into the grievous predicament of slavery (Matt. 18:25). Others from among the poor found themselves imprisoned, only to see the free world again after members of their family had paid off their debts (Matt. 18:30). Jesus likely witnessed many Jews fall into the wretched world of poverty and enslavement as a result of debts. That is doubtless why Jesus recognized poverty as causing hunger, begging, robbery, sickness, social estrangement, imprisonment, and enslavement (Isa. 58:5-7; 60:1-2; Luke 4:18-19; 16:20).[25]

Although no precise dating of Jesus' life and ministry is determinable from the biblical and extrabiblical sources, Jesus was likely born and lived at about the time of the reign of the Roman emperors Augustus and Tiberius. In other words, Jesus was likely born toward the end of Herod the Great's rule, just prior to 4 B.C.E. Jesus, who came from a large family, likely participated in the religiously significant events of Jewish faith (Matt. 13:55). Jesus, raised in the Jewish tradition, probably engaged in Jerusalem festivals during the Passover (recalling the Exodus), the Pentecost (recalling God's ownership of the productive land), and the Feast of Booths (an eight-day harvest festival recalling forty years in the wilderness).

Jesus was not only born in the period of Roman rule over Palestinian society, but was killed by Romans who claimed the right to impose capital punishment.[26] The execution of Jesus was decreed by the procurator Pilate and Herod Antipas (Luke 23:1-12). The Gospels do implicate the political and religious authorities in the decision to bring Jesus' life to an end on the cross.[27] Some Christians believe Jesus was a spiritual teacher disinterested in politics and social change; yet, Jesus was not crucified from a misunderstanding, but from action taken by authorities who saw their social order endangered. Indeed, the cross was used primarily on dissidents whose activities threatened established economic and political interests.

The Humanity and Ministry of the Hard-Hitting Jesus

Mainline Christians often prefer to focus on the Christ of dogma who is known as the Lord of the universe, savior of the world, and firstborn of all creation.[28] Such a theological focus annuls the real humanity of the hard-hitting Jesus that is an essential aspect of God's revelation on the cross. The Jesus of Nazareth who lived for others exhibits a genuine humanity with all of its limitation. The hard-hitting Jesus felt joy, grief, anger, solitude, temptation, conflict, prayer, hunger, thirst, pity, kindness, fear, and death.[29] According to Luke, Jesus experienced the developmental process and "increased in wisdom and in years, and in divine and human favor" (2:52). Jesus' suffering on the cross bears witness to his humanity.

Jesus' ministry both attracted a large following and alienated Pharisees, scribes, rich Jews, Zealots, Sadducees, and priests.[30] Jesus offended the wealthy by asking them to give their possessions to the poor. Landowners and wealthy families rejected Jesus for saying, "It is easier for a camel to go through the eye of a needle than for someone who is rich to enter the kingdom of God" (Mark 10:25). Moreover, in the context of his ministry, he offended pious Jews and officials when he gathered and ate with despised tax collectors and the unclean. Zealots expected Jesus to militantly reject the Roman occupying powers and those that served Rome. The chief priests and Sadducees who profited from the Temple economy considered Jesus a problem.

The Cross and the Humiliated

The hard-hitting Jesus who revealed God on the cross questioned all social, political, cultural, and religious orders that claimed to control access to the truth of God. The hard-hitting Jesus, tempted to embrace the traditional messianic expectations of his people, rejected the will to political domination, religious power, and material security (Luke 4:1-13; Matt. 4:1-11). This Jesus lived out his call in suffering, service, and death—the way of the cross. The hard-hitting Jesus fully revealed the saving love of God that converts human beings to the way of justice. The powerlessness of the Crucified God is the love that changes deaths to life in the barrio, in the Rio Grande crossings to El Norte, or massacres by soldiers on village streets.

From the time of temptation in the wilderness, Jesus refused to reduce the saving love of God to a display of power.[31] He walked with the humiliated and powerless of the world, even dying like one of them on a cross. Still, people seem always to desire displays of supernatural power, the witness of love. When Jesus was on the cross the people around him said, "let him come down from the cross now, and we will believe in him" (Matt. 27:42). The hard-hitting Jesus knows faith and conversion lead people to find God in their lives. Hence, through his cross the mysterious meaning of God's love in the world is made known. That love does not kill the Son on the cross; instead, the cross reveals the love of a parent who suffers the legally sanctioned death of a child. The silence of God on the cross is a sign of God's solidarity with human beings who are free to follow God toward the kingdom of new life or kill God in their world of sin.

The Passion

Christians refer to the suffering and death of Jesus as "the passion." *Passion* is derived from the Latin word *patior*, which means "to suffer" or "take on." Suffering was imposed on Jesus by the hostile ruling authorities that put him to death; yet, he also endured torment for the sake of his mission and the gospel of God. I am particularly moved by Mark's Gospel that tells us that imperial triumph is not the last word about Jesus' death; instead, death on the cross is seen as a consequence of Jesus' liberating practice and message. I think Christians will find themselves particularly moved by the passion narrative in the Gospel of Mark (14:1–15:47). Conspiracy and betrayal highlight the story of Jesus' arrest, trial, and death.

Early in Mark's account, readers learn that Jesus' public ministry was opposed (3:6), thus we are prepared for the plot to kill Jesus devised by the priests and scribes in Jerusalem (11:17-18). Mark leaves little room for doubt that a distinct connection exists between Jesus' death and his public action. Mark's Jesus predicts his violent death three times (8:31; 9:31; 10:33-34) before disciples who cannot understand. Why did Jesus go to Jerusalem knowing death awaited him? Jerusalem was the theological center of Jewish society where concerns about salvation were focused in the Temple. The prophetic literature centered attention on this holy city and Jewish identity was tied to its fate.[32] Jesus went to Jerusalem to perish like a prophet (Luke 13:33).

Mark tells us in the passion narrative that the journey to the cross takes place during the high holy days in Jerusalem. Indeed, the chief priests and scribes began their plot to kill Jesus when it was just "two days before the Passover and the festival of Unleavened Bread" (Mark 14:1). Jesus was in the house of Simon the leper in Bethany as the authorities conspired with a fallen disciple named Judas to arrest Jesus. That Jesus was in the house of a social outcast points to his enduring challenge to society's rigid barriers. Just before his arrest, a woman whose name is not made known recognized that Jesus was destined to die. She anointed him with oil valued at a laborer's yearly wage, even though the disciples protested her action (Mark 14:8).

Naturally, the disciples wanted to sell the oil and use the money for the poor; yet, Jesus praised the woman's actions and told the disciples to leave her alone. Curiously, Jesus said, "For you always have the poor with you, and you can show kindness to them whenever you wish; but you will not always have me" (Mark 14:7). Some Christians wrongly think Jesus is here legitimating poverty as a unchanging way of life. Stress needs to be put on the idea that the disciples will not always have Jesus. In other words, the time for Jesus to die had come and the woman knew it. That a woman anointed Jesus points to her assuming a role of utter importance. The nameless woman knew Jesus was about to take up the cross. Unlike the disciples, she stood with him.[33]

Mainline church members should not be surprised when their Latino brothers and sisters grasp certain elements in the passion narrative not interpreted by them. For instance, the Last Supper scene (Mark 14:12-25) reflects a message best understood in contexts of persecution and injustice. That Jesus secretly prepared for the Passover meal with the disciples is apparent from the instructions given to the disciples, "Go into the city, and a man carrying a jar of water will meet you; follow him, and wherever he enters, say to the owner of the house, 'The Teacher asks, Where is my guest room, where I may eat the Passover with my disciples?'" (Mark 14:13-14). Jesus and his followers were underground in Jerusalem, communicating with a network of people in symbolic ways.

Jesus shared a farewell meal with his disciples in a "safehouse." Jesus knew the upper room's security was precarious and predicted that one of the twelve would betray him (Mark 14:17-21). He further accused all the disciples of wavering in their solidarity with the cross. Indeed, Peter would deny Jesus three times and all the disciples would finally flee (Mark 14:26-31). Jesus' parting meal, nonetheless, draws attention toward his messianic mission.[34] Remember the reign of God was earlier made known to hungry crowds by Jesus (Mark 6:41; 8:6). He gathered a diverse people into community in the wilderness, presenting God's reign as a feast held with the outcast. The Last Supper alluded to the new order of life for which Jesus would die (Mark 14:25; Luke 14:15-24).

Jesus offered a blessing over the bread and cup from which the disciples drank. That cup images Jesus' suffering witness before the powerful.[35] Drinking from it implied entering into a radical solidarity with the way of the cross. Solidarity with the way of the cross includes joining with the powerless against the injustices of the powerful. At the Last Supper, Jesus taught his stumbling disciples the importance of taking up the cross. He likely echoed the Mount of Olives discourse where he said, "they will hand you over to councils; and you will be beaten in synagogues; and you will stand before governors and kings because of me, as a testimony to them" (Mark 13:9-11). Taking the cup means bearing witness to the truth of God.

Meanwhile, the conspirators, concerned not to alert the crowds who favored Jesus, enlisted Judas, who was one of the twelve, to betray Jesus. Judas gave his back to Jesus for material reasons. Money, not Jesus, was important to Judas. Judas led soldiers who carried swords and clubs to the Mount of Olives to arrest Jesus. Judas is the "insider" who identified Jesus with a kiss so the authorities could arrest Jesus. The arrest was carefully executed so the public would not notice.[36] Religious leaders thought it was necessary to be rid of Jesus because he did the work of the devil, raised insolent questions of Israel's leaders and criticized religious authorities, lacked respect for the law and the Temple, and made otherwise uninspired people rebellious.

The chief priests, scribes, and ordinary pious people offered only a crown of thorns to the messiah who asked the question, "Who do people say that I am?" (Mark 8:27-33). Indeed, religious, political and national forces acted in concert to bring about Jesus' death. In a courtroom, Jesus is condemned to die. Those in power reject the God revealed by Jesus who favors the poor, women, and unclean people. Religious authorities not only wanted their categories of belonging recognized, but they insisted that the Temple was still the place to meet God. Jesus made plain that despised and unclean people reveal God sooner than God could be found at the Temple (Luke 10:25-37; Matt. 25:31-46). Jesus spoke the truth, only to succumb to a judicial murder ordered by the powerful.[37] Society's God was more important to the powerful than the God of love who gives life to rejected people.

Thus, in the Holy City Jesus is branded a blasphemer by the Sanhedrin or Jewish council, which had ruling power over religious and civil matters. That Jesus is tried before the full Sanhedrin at night evidences how mainline religious officials were not above breaking their own religious rules (Mark 14:55; Matt. 26:59). Although trials were not to be held at night, on the Sabbath, or during Passover, mainline religious officials dispensed with the requirements. False evidence was presented against Jesus merely to strengthen the council's pre-made decision. Principally, Jesus was accused of saying he would destroy the Temple and rebuild it in three days (Mark 14:58). Jesus must die. He was a blasphemer who threatened the social order (Mark 14:64) and its concept of God.

Once convicted, Jesus was beaten and humiliated at the hands of the mainline religious authorities. When the threat of repressive power was thought too near, Jesus was socially abandoned by those closest to him (Mark 14:68; Matt. 14:50). The council consulted the following morning and then took Jesus to Pilate who asked, "Are you the King of the Jews?" (Mark 15:2). Jesus was also degraded by Gentiles who mockingly crowned him with thorns and dressed him in purple Roman cloaks, a symbol of imperialist power.[38] Jesus' witness to God contradicted the mainline religious understanding of a God who favors the privileged and powerful; moreover, the inscription on the cross, "Jesus of Nazareth, the King of the Jews" (John 19:19), indicates he threatened the political order.

Paradoxically, Jesus was killed by powerful economic and political interests in God's name. Jesus was taken to be crucified at Golgotha—a defiled place. The mainline religious officials who took Jesus to the cross were utterly convinced they were doing the will of God. Feeling vindicated by Jesus' suffering on the cross, the mainline religious leaders would mockingly say, "He saved others; he cannot save himself" (Mark 15:31). Meanwhile, the Romans, who killed a mere political agitator, believed the cross would deter other challenges to their power over Jewish society. Indeed, the cross was intended to disclaim the authority of Jesus and to warn followers. On the cross Jesus' mission appeared to have met defeat.

Interestingly, the mainline religious tradition of Jesus' day held to the idea that God is essentially expressed in the world as power; however, the crucified Jesus discloses God in the world in suffering love. Contemplating God's abandonment of Jesus on the cross makes us call into question ideas of God that are disconnected from the concrete world of those who are oppressed by systems of evil and left alone to die. What does the abandonment of the Son mean? Certainly, it tells us that God fully enters the world of tortured and rejected human beings. Jesus, abandoned by God on the cross, expresses love by becoming solidarized with all in human society and individual existence that negates life and promotes injustice for human beings. God so loves the world that God allows human beings to place God at their mercy.

The crucified Jesus' words to the pious are, "This generation may be charged with the blood of all the prophets" (Luke 11:50). Indeed, many religious people sided with the mainline religious officials who damned Jesus to death. They likely believed in the correctness of the verdict, especially when Jesus was crying out as one whose mission had failed, "My God, my God, why have you forsaken me?" (Mark 15:34; Ps. 22). It may be easier to accept the idea that civil and religious authorities put Jesus to death on the cross; however, the fact that Jesus suffered the torment of the cross while bitterly crying out to a God who does not answer is very troubling. Still, the God who abandoned Jesus drew suffering and death into the internal structure of God on the cross. Again, God's silence directs us to God's pain that comes from our freedom to act against God.

How do we understand the silence of God before the despairing cry of Jesus?[39] The synoptic Gospels report that for a period of three hours darkness fell over the whole land (Mark 15:33; Matt. 27:45-50; Luke 23:44-46). This reference reminds one of Yahweh's blotting out of the sun in Egypt to register a blow against a world order that needed slaves

(Exod. 10:22).[40] God's response to the mainline religious tradition that celebrated the absence of God to Jesus on the cross is clear. When Jesus died, the Temple veil covering the entrance to the Holy Place was torn in two from top to bottom. Jesus' death radically critiqued the mainline religious tradition by subverting the idea that access to God was mediated by the Temple and the established social order.

On the cross, God was separated from a mainline religious system whose leaders claimed the right to define God. On the cross all prior notions about God uttered by those who wished to maintain systems of domination in the world were negated. Jesus was abandoned by God on the cross to show that God saves by incarnation in the suffering and death of human beings. Indeed, God "so loved the world that [God] gave [God's] only Son" (John 3:16). God leads human beings who freely participate in evil systems to life by putting before them the experience of Jesus abandoned on the cross. Finally, after Jesus was dead, a Roman soldier and a member of the Sanhedrin negated their support systems to acknowledge the God who assumes the sin, torment, and death of humanity (Mark 15:39, 43).

Women Take Up the Cross

The women who followed and served the poor with Jesus throughout the Galilean ministry went to Jerusalem. Although the repressive power of the state and religion endangered their lives, Mary Magdalene, Mary the mother of James, and Salome did not flee the authorities. They witnessed Jesus dying on the cross. Women were social nobodies who were excluded from the enterprise of interpreting faith. The mainline religious tradition symbolically devalued them in relation to God;[41] yet, women prove more faithful than their culturally privileged male counterparts to the call of the cross. Neither members of the mainline religious tradition nor culturally privileged males are first chosen to convey the message of the Resurrection (Mark 15:40; 16:1-8).

In other words, that women are with Jesus at his hour of death once again uncommonly locates the gospel in the world of the lowly and excluded (Mark 16:10). The women who were the first witnesses to the empty tomb quickly recognized that Jesus' death on the cross reveals the power of life-giving love. Women link the story of Jesus' passion and the reality of the Resurrection. Their lips first utter that life comes from death, especially for those who take up the way of the cross and are crucified by worldly systems for the cause of justice. Today, there are women in many places who courageously take up the living cross of Jesus by defending the rights of the least members of the community.

In El Salvador I met women who had willingly taken up the cross for the sake of the gospel. In the late 1970s and early 1980s, hundreds of people began to disappear or their tortured bodies were found on country roads. Salvadoran mothers experienced the pain of having a family member disappear or be killed at the hands of the official government. Political repression and human cruelty toward the poor took the form of crucifixion manifested as many people turning up dead each day. As Salvadoran mothers shared their pain about losing their children and loved ones, they decided to take up the cross by organizing COMADRES (Committee of the Mothers and Relatives of Political Prisoners, Disappeared, and Assassinated of El Salvador, Monseñor Oscar Arnulfo Romero).

For the women of COMADRES, taking up the cross means giving one's life for Jesus who was crucified for the hope of the poor and outcast. These Salvadoran women tell us that greatness in a world of crucified people means taking on the suffering of those denied social justice. The living cross means working for justice. The women of COMADRES reveal God hidden in the suffering of the poor who call us to love one another. I remember Patricia testifying in a room filled with the names and pictures of persons who had been killed or who had disappeared. Patricia was arrested with a friend who was injured by riot police at a civil demonstration organized by COMADRES that called the Salvadoran government to account for political prisoners, the disappeared, and the murdered.

Suffering was engraved on Patricia's face as she described her ordeal in one of El Salvador's clandestine jails. A bag was placed over her head and she was taken to a military base. She was stripped of her clothing and severely beaten by soldiers who used their fists, feet, and rifle butts.

Soldiers took turns raping her and declaring they would kill her in the end. After several days of torture and rape, Patricia's hands were tied by the thumbs behind her back and she was dumped into the trunk of a car. Soldiers drove her to a secluded place where, in return for her life, she was asked to denounce COMADRES as a guerrilla organization. Terrified, Patricia waited for the soldiers to kill her.

Patricia refused to lie about COMADRES. She told the soldiers to kill her. "COMADRES is not a guerrilla group but is made up of a group of mothers devoted to defending human rights. I cannot lie. You might as well kill me." Again, the soldiers took her back to the clandestine jail where they administered electric shock to Patricia's body. After more beatings and rape by the soldiers, Patricia was again blindfolded and placed in a cold, stainless steel room. Patricia crawled naked around the floor, aware that soldiers were still in the cell with her. There was a smell of putrefying blood in the room. As she felt her way around the floor, her hand touched a finger, a piece of an arm, and a limbless torso. Her face looked terrified beneath the blindfold.

Frantically, she crawled around the room trying to find a head to determine whether or not the quartered body was her injured friend. Suddenly, a soldier called out, "That is what we are going to do to you and to your family, if you don't admit that COMADRES is a guerrilla organization." Patricia was afraid for her family, but the cross of Jesus empowered her to confront her tormenters. Again, she refused to bring false testimony against COMADRES and told the soldiers to go ahead and kill her. Frustrated, the soldiers said, "This woman is not afraid of anything!" Her life was spared only because the international solidarity movement pressured the government for her release. Tearfully, Patricia declared that international solidarity saved her life.

Like the women who first witnessed the resurrection of Jesus, Patricia declares that no human evil can overcome the power of God's love in the world. Patricia, who experienced life in a clandestine jail, was strong in the power of the cross. Indeed, for the women of COMADRES, the cross of Jesus basically conveys both a message of hope and a condemnation of the sin of the world. That is why it is termed a living cross. Confronted with the scandal of sin, suffering, and death at the hands of soldiers, Patricia knew that life was the future promise of God who died on the cross. She was faithful to the God who resurrected the murdered Son. Faith assured her that the struggle for justice and love waged by the abandoned of this world shall reign in the end.

Losing Life to Find It

As money and power produce more competent forms of violence against human beings in the world, Christians need to reflect anew on the meaning of the cross for their identity in the world. The cross points to the violence of human beings and of their social institutions. North American churches must find God on the cross—the symbol of divine nearness to places of pain and violent rejection. Mainline churches that rediscover their identity in the cross willingly surrender their lives by taking on the burdens and struggles of suffering and abandoned people. Christians who seek the Crucified Lord in society will find him with the socially abused, the murdered, the racially hated, and the economically destitute of an ever more familiar global context.

Mainline Christians must admit that only in the Crucified God will they see their future disclosed. The Gospels and the testimony of Christians tell us that the crucified Jesus points to God, present within the history of all people whose cries and pain judge human cruelty as acts of savagery against God. What does it mean to lose life in order to find it on the cross? It means mainline churches will use their resources to build communities that function as centers of life for social outcasts who only know abandonment, social injustice, poverty, suffering, and death. It means proclaiming to the larger culture that the ongoing crucifixion of people in history must yield to God's purposes for humanity and nature.

Jesus, who is crucified each day by human violence and economic systems that make people poor, communicates a new understanding of God (1 Cor. 1:18–2:5). From the cross Jesus shows God is free of human categories of understanding; indeed, human wisdom is idolatrous when it claims absolute knowledge of God. In the crucified Jesus, who is the foundation of Christian understanding in the world, God transcends all anthropological limitations. Because the

God who suffers and dies also saves, the historical point of departure for human redemption begins in the setting of the weak and power-less. As mainline Christians confront the suffering of a world long-ing for liberation, they should remember that God is always hidden in the drama of the weak and human crucifixion.

Without doubt, the answer to Jesus' question "Who do people say that I am?" is the word of the cross backed by the reality of resurrec-tion. Mainline Christians declare that their risen Lord is "Jesus of Nazareth, who was crucified" (Mark 16:6). The risen Carpenter is the one who preached conversion to the kingdom of God at hand and good news to the poor and outcast. The risen Christ is Jesus of Nazareth who unmasked the abuses of the powerful and suffered per-secution and death at their hands. Jesus, who suffered abandonment, is also the first one risen by God. He is remembered in the earliest Christian discourses as "the Holy and Righteous One" (Acts 3:14). Through the witness of the Resurrection, the cross says that God rejects human criminality and gives life.

In our society, places of crucifixion are found in the barrio where a crucified people live. From that place of marginality and premature death, a new voice speaks to North American society about the Crucified God and people. Specifically, the word of the cross and the hope of the Resurrection are enfleshed in the social history of Salvadoran refugees who are now living in the barrio. These brothers and sisters of the crucified Jesus encourage mainline Christians and native Latino residents in "completing what is lacking in Christ's afflictions" (Col. 1:24). Listening to these Latinos may result in an evangelized mainline church converted to the world of those not counted among the notable.

Notes

1. Bernard Lohse, *A Short History of Christian Doctrine* (Philadelphia: Fortress Press, 1978), pp. 52-53.
2. *The United Methodist Hymnal* (Nashville: Abingdon Press, 1989), p. 881.
3. Jürgen Moltmann, *The Crucified God* (New York: Harper & Row, 1974), pp. 37-39.

4. Leonardo Boff, *Passion of Christ, Passion of the World* (Maryknoll, N.Y.: Orbis Books, 1987), p. 11.

5. Richard Horsley, *Jesus and the Spiral of Violence: Popular Jewish Resistance in Roman Palestine* (Philadelphia: Fortress Press, 1993), p. 3.

6. Ibid.

7. R. David Kaylor, *Jesus the Prophet: His Vision of the Kingdom on Earth* (Louisville: Westminster/John Knox Press, 1994), p. 47.

8. M. Stern, "The Reign of Herod and the Herodian Dynasty," in *The Jewish People in the First Century,* vol. 1, ed. S. Safrai and M. Stern (Assen, The Netherlands: Van Gorcum and Comp. B.V., 1974), p. 240.

9. M. Stern, "The Reign of Herod and the Herodian Dynasty," p. 227.

10. Horsley, *Jesus and the Spiral of Violence,* p. 44.

11. Henk Jagersma, *A History of Israel from Alexander the Great to Bar Kochba* (Philadelphia: Fortress Press, 1986), pp. 108-9.

12. Horsley, *Jesus and the Spiral of Violence,* pp. 73-77.

13. See Henk Jagersma, *A History of Israel from Alexander the Great to Bar Kochba,* p. 111; M. Stern, "The Reign of Herod and the Herodian Dynasty," p. 277.

14. Stern, "The Reign of Herod and the Herodian Dynasty," pp. 277-78.

15. Horsley, *Jesus and the Spiral of Violence,* pp. 50-51.

16. Stern, "The Reign of Herod and the Herodian Dynasty," pp. 279-80.

17. Jagersma, *A History of Israel from Alexander the Great to Bar Kochba,* p. 115.

18. Stern, "The Reign of Herod and the Herodian Dynasty," p. 283.

19. Kaylor, *Jesus the Prophet,* p. 26.

20. Ibid., p. 27.

21. Jagersma, *A History of Israel from Alexander the Great to Bar Kochba,* p. 119.

22. Ibid.

23. Ibid., pp. 119-20.

24. See Ched Meyers, *Binding the Strong Man: A Political Reading of Mark's Story of Jesus* (Maryknoll, N.Y.: Orbis Books, 1988), p. 308. William R. Herzog II, *Parables as Subversive Speech: Jesus as Pedagogue of the Oppressed* (Louisville: Westminster/John Knox Press, 1994), chapter 6.

25. See Jon Sobrino, *Jesus in Latin America* (Maryknoll, N.Y.: Orbis Books, 1987), p. 90.

26. John Dominic Crossan, *The Historical Jesus: The Life of a Mediterranean Jewish Peasant* (San Francisco: HarperSanFrancisco, 1992), p. 372.

27. Kaylor, *Jesus the Prophet,* p. 50.

28. See Boff, *Passion of Christ, Passion of the World;* Hayes, John H., *Son of God to Super Star: Twentieth-Century Interpretations of Jesus* (Nashville: Abingdon Press, 1976); and Song, *Jesus, The Crucified People.*

29. See Boff, *Passion of Christ, Passion of the World.*

30. Horsley, *Jesus and the Spiral of Violence: Popular Jewish Resistance in Roman Palestine;* and Meyers, *Binding the Strong Man.*

31. Boff, *Passion of Christ, Passion of the World* (Maryknoll, N.Y.: Orbis Books, 1993), p. 15.

32. Virgilio Elizondo, *Galilean Journey* (Maryknoll, N.Y.: Orbis Books, 1983), p. 68.

33. Meyers, *Binding the Strong Man: A Political Reading of Mark's Story of Jesus* (Maryknoll, N.Y.: Orbis Books, 1988), p. 359.

34. Donald Senior, *The Passion of Jesus in the Gospel of Mark* (Collegeville, Minn.: Michael Glazier, 1984), p. 54.

35. Meyers, *Binding the Strong Man*, p. 362.

36. Ibid., p. 360.

37. Boff, *Passion of Christ, Passion of the World*, p. 41.

38. Meyers, *Binding the Strong Man*, p. 379.

39. See especially Moltmann, *The Crucified God*.

40. Meyers, *Binding the Strong Man*, p. 388.

41. See especially Gerda Lerner, *The Creation of Patriarchy* (New York: Oxford University Press, 1986), chapter 9.

Chapter Four

The Struggle
of a Crucified People

Untroubled Theologians

they find new ways to
speak of their ignorance

with an authority that
chooses not to welcome

those blunt questions that
strut inevitably about in

life like a dance straining
any body of truth. what

wisdom of sacred things
is found on the lips of

the forgotten or the
upraised fists of people

left to die on roads
where vultures feast is

scarcely ever entertained
as intelligence of faith

pointing to God resident
in every crime against

humanity and this world
to humility raped. with any

luck they might see over
their babble now beyond the

minefields of the academy
the Lord will not deliver

life to death even
when those who most

call his name in
comfort are met with

certain silence.

North American cultural pluralism makes plain that in human experience objects of thought such as God, nature, and society are never known directly, entirely, or in the raw. Human speech and symbols meaningfully depict these objects as cultural facts shaped and amended by history. Because mainline Christianity is part of a global environment defined by cultural and religious pluralism, those who judge theological truth by its relation to the gospel are not asked to interpret their piety by excluding or attacking other cultural readings of the sacred. Today, members of mainline churches are requested to enter into a dialogue with persons from the barrio who represent Latino culture.

Why is cross-cultural dialogue important? Mainline churches are pressed more than ever to take cultures seriously in order to extend the future life of their churches. Dialogue between communities of separate or different faith convictions will typify faith reflection in the future. Among others, mainline Protestant Christians will need to face other cultural viewpoints in their contrast and divergence. In other words, members of mainline churches will need to walk with diverse cultures to survey anew the basis for the theological assertion of God's sovereignty and relation to moral understanding and the created world. Time will have to be devoted to observing how contextually mediated social, political, economic, and cultural processes finally shape theological judgments.

Awareness of cultural diversity implies recognition that global religions are cultural systems of knowledge that mold and reshape meaning in differing social settings where people act to create their identity. Mainline Christians need to view the world's different forms of Christianity and other religions as expressions of specific cultural communities and a ground of divine revelation. Modern self-awareness compels a formal link between particular faith experiences and the many ways that human beings express their deepest questions and ultimate hope. Mainline Christians who step out of the absolute confidence of dominant culture will enter a world where faith is a struggle to clarify where it stands in the scheme of contrasting cultural experiences.

No one can deny that the "global picture" of Christianity shows a plurality of cultural styles. The Latino religious world alone affirms the belief that "God spoke to our ancestors in many and various ways" (Heb. 1:1). Although the Latino faith expressions previously found in the barrio and those that are being carried into it today by new Latino groups have been largely ignored by the dominant culture, Latino interpretations of the gospel are undeniably part of universal Christianity's theological terrain. Throughout the 1980s mainline Christians were overcoming their alienation from these readings of the faith tradition by listening to Latinos who asserted that Christ died outside the gate to give all life.

For instance, for over a decade, mainline churches' progressive wings were particularly solidarized with the political struggles of the poor of El Salvador and their Salvadoran counterparts in the United

States. The solidarity movement was a genuine reflection of a new way of thinking about God and the Scriptures. Mainline Christians did theology from below by reading the Scriptures from the perspective of the oppressed, giving sanctuary to Salvadoran and Guatemalan refugees, and demanding an end to the U.S. government's involvement in Central American civil wars. Mainline churches' contact with Latinos issued forth in an alternative understanding of the political conflict in Central America that featured issues of wealth and poverty.

Although Central Americans and Salvadorans are now living in cities all across the United States, mainline churches are presently ignoring them. Salvadorans have simply become another group of "hispanics" in the States that are simply no longer seen as a moral focus in mainline church life. Because many progressive mainline Christians believe that peace and democracy are being established in El Salvador, their ethical interests have turned to other long-neglected matters. Indeed, mainline denominations are replacing social gospel interests with a new privatized Christianity that emphasizes personal spirituality. The faithful are increasingly evacuating the world of political conflicts to build a more subjectively grounded church.

Nevertheless, Latinos are giving voice to a prophetic agenda for society from the barrios of U.S. cities. Specifically, Salvadoran refugees are one group that speak to us of alternative values and practices from the perspective of the poor and oppressed. Salvadoran refugees living in U.S. cities heighten social awareness of unjust structural, historical, and ethical matters reflective of international actuality. According to the 1990 census, there are 565,000 Salvadorans in the United States. Immigrants rights groups estimate a population of one million. The latter may be the more accurate figure. They have a great deal to tell us about the ethical renewal of mainline Christianity in the heart of a nation that claims to live under God.

Why devote time to the Salvadoran story? We must recognize that Salvadorans share with other Latino populations in the United States the status of marginality and a situation of inequality in relation to the larger culture. They also share the ethnic label "hispanic"; moreover, among U.S. Latino groups, Salvadorans have been largely voiceless within socially empowering structures. In particular, Black, White, and U.S. Latino societies need to hear the story of this voiceless and rejected ethnic group. Finally, the Salvadoran story has profound theological value because it draws the attention of all Christians to a particular people and location in history that reveals the universal and ongoing contextual revelation of the Crucified God.

Indeed, for most Salvadorans living overseas or in the United States, life is filled with insecurity and hardship. Salvadorans have found the strength to live under miserable conditions in the hope of the Crucified God. North American religious communities struggling to find new life in the gospel will discover that faith and Christian hope have fortified Salvadorans and given them life. At the theological level, the story of the Salvadoran people reminds Christians in the United States that the message of Jesus is a source of resistance to oppression, a light that opens a path to a new humanity, and a transforming word before life's deepest horrors. It will not hurt to find the Crucified God incarnate in the life of the Salvadoran people.

Economic Migrants? Political Refugees?

What was going on in the 1980s? In the 1980s there was a sharp increase in international migration from Central America, stemming from repressive governments and contracting economies. Population exchanges in the past between the United States and Central America were economically motivated; however, the U.S. was now unprepared or unwilling to admit the political motives behind the movement of peoples across the border. The U.S. government denied Salvadorans official recognition as political refugees. Meanwhile, in the States, cultural discourse about non-native born Latinos negatively defined Salvadorans as "illegal aliens" who deserved to be sent back to where they came from.[1]

The explicit histories of Salvadoran refugees who had questioned the actions of the U.S. government in Central America challenged the alienating public discourse. Yet, Salvadoran refugee arrivals were not conceptually constituted by the myth of a "nation of immigrants" and "refugees" able and ready to provide safe haven to the persecuted. Exclusion of newcomers is not new. In 1882 the Chinese Exclusion Act was passed, although repealed when China and the United States united to fight Japan. The first restrictive immigration act was passed in 1875. By the 1920s, national origins quota acts were introduced to limit immigration to the States from specific geographic areas. Finally, the term "illegal immigrant" was coined and statistics kept on these people.[2]

Salvadorans once migrated to the States for mostly economic reasons. By the late 1970s, political friction had deepened in El Salvador and innocent people were being killed by soldiers. Since 1980, open civil war and subsequent economic deterioration have formed the basic reasons why Salvadoran refugees leave their home country.[3] Only 17 percent of the one million Salvadorans living in the States had migrated from El Salvador by 1977. After 1979 when political friction sharpened the crisis of Salvadoran society, more than three-fourths of the current total population of one million came to the U.S.[4]

In North American barrios, Salvadoran refugees interpret their lives through the symbolic system of a popular religion that relates belief and behavior to struggles for justice. *Struggle* is defined in the context of a culture of protest as a battle against the repressive Salvadoran political regime in the interest of establishing a democratized political order in El Salvador. The popular religion brought to the United States by Salvadoran refugees supplies new social and political values for society that motivate social change. From the barrios of North American society, Salvadoran refugees give voice to the social and material concerns of the majority poor who have been excluded from the political and economic structures of society.

Salvadorans are new Latino residents of the barrio who speak of a religion of martyrology. The religion of martyrology speaks to the prophetic concerns of the church universal as it reflects changes in both the balance of State power in El Salvador and the United States. The Salvadoran religion of martyrology actuates an ethic of protest and struggle in Christians. For these rejected newcomers to U.S. society, martyrdom does not mean risking persecution, torture, and death explicitly for the sake of faith. Martyrdom communicates a prophetic message centered on striving against injustice and political repression. Salvadorans influenced by the religion of martyrology sacrifice personal life in the struggle to change unjust economic and political structures in society.

First, I want to situate the religion of martyrology in Salvadoran cultural history where it exists as a knowledge system that forms and reshapes cultural meaning in contexts of unequal power and domination. Second, I will point out the characteristic feature of the religion of martyrology, showing how it conveys cultural meaning in contexts and through discourse that critiques the economic and political violence in El Salvador and the United States. Third, I will indicate that our Salvadoran brothers and sisters remind us through their faith views of the hard-hitting Jesus' claim on all of our lives. Because the Salvadoran story of crucifixion includes U.S. government involvement, North Americans are morally accountable to this community.

The Coffee Boom Begins Modern History

What sets modern Salvadoran history in motion is nothing other than coffee. Salvadoran coffee production went up as the beverage's popularity rose in the North Atlantic community. By the 1850s, coffee plantations expanded in response to international market demands.[5] Once the landed elite realized the economic value of coffee, the agrarian structure of El Salvador was recast. New demands were made of the land, which produced novel social relations that favored the ruling class over the masses, who were pushed into want. Undoubtedly, modern Salvadoran agro-export and oligarchical rule are linked to those cups of coffee enjoyed in coffee shops in El Norte.

By the mid–nineteenth century, the oligarchic government of El Salvador gave coffee production legislative support, which instituted sweeping changes in the land tenure system. Between 1879 and 1881, legislation was passed that eliminated all the systems of Indian-based communal land. Mostly, Salvadoran native peoples were dispossessed of their holdings by legal mechanisms that permitted land to be amassed by a small subdivision of Euro-Latino society made up of about 250 families. The legislative-based cancellation of the communal lands created an economic structure that secured the best land for wealthy Salvadorans while pushing powerless natives into destitution.

The state served the interest of the coffee-growing sector by developing the domestic infrastructure and keeping social order through military repression within the national boundaries. Already, at this early point in time, required labor and rural order were obtained with the aid of security forces. Native American people whose struggle against land dispossession dates back to the arrival of the Spanish in the early 1500s were not passive. Annulment of communal landholdings caused divested Indian groups in the western part of the country to rebel repeatedly between 1872 and 1898.[6] Still, their revolts were no match for the ascending and near homogeneous dominant class that was able to mobilize the repressive power of the state.[7]

For instance, El Salvador's first great political trauma came on December 21, 1931, after a small group of junior army officers initiated a coup that turned over formal government power to General Maximiliano Hernandez Martinez. This marked the start of the longest unbroken military rule in the history of any nation in Latin America. Between 1932 and 1979 El Salvador had seventeen military governments.[8] Interestingly, General Martinez, referred to as *El Brujo* (The Warlock) for his occult practices, was the military strongman who inspired Gabriel Garcia Marquez's *The Autumn of the Patriarch*. He revered Benito Mussolini and Adolf Hitler. Because he believed in the principle of reincarnation, human life was for him more expendable than that of an ant whose death was eternal.

In 1932, General Martinez used his power to initiate *la matanza* (massacre). A series of uprisings took place in the western part of the country that Martinez brutally repressed. Miguel Mármol, who survived an execution attempt by government forces, said of the massacre: "I believe that the drama of 1932 is for El Salvador what the Nazi barbarity was for Europe, what the North American barbarity was for Viet Nam. . . . El Salvador is today the work of that barbarity."[9] About 2 percent (30,000) of the total national population was killed. Ethnicity played a role as those killed were mostly Indian. An ethnic massacre of that scale in the States would mean killing about four hundred thousand of the twenty million Latino residents.

Modernization and Social Protest

The Cuban revolution (1959) inspired both increased government repression and more militant popular opposition. In the 1960s, the United States, concerned to avoid another Cuba, strengthened the Salvadoran police and armed forces to combat the communist threat. Because land reform was equated with communism by the landed oligarchy, the U.S. ignored that crucial issue. Although no guerrilla threat in El Salvador existed, the United States advanced counterinsurgency programs alongside those of economic development. Because structural inequities were increasing and creating bitter conditions of life for the majority population of El Salvador, the U.S. government anticipated a potential for civil violence. In 1967, a U.S. Public Safety Program report stated:

> The Public Safety Program in El Salvador is 10 years old and the advisors have efficiently trained the [Salvadoran] National Guard and National Police in basic tactics so that authorities have been successful in handling any politically motivated demonstrations in recent years. . . . With the potential danger that exists in a densely populated country where the rich are very rich and the poor extremely poor, El Salvador is fortunate that the Guard and the Police are well trained and disciplined.[10]

Government repression deepened when the head of the Salvadoran National Guard, General Jose Medrano, President Fidel Sanchez Hernandez, and U.S. advisors founded the Democratic Nationalist Organization (ORDEN [Spanish for order]). ORDEN, founded in the late-1960s, was a zealous anticommunist paramilitary force of an estimated eighty thousand to one hundred thousand members. ORDEN members were tied to the military government by a patronage system, carried weapons, acted with impunity, and functioned as an informant network to ensure control in rural zones. ORDEN, a precursor of the "death squads" to surface in the 1970s, spawned El Salvador's first "death squad," the White Hand.[11]

Between the 1960s and 1970s, popular organizations surfaced as alternative vehicles for social change by demanding better living conditions and land redistribution. Several political parties were organized to contest the hegemony of the military party or National Conciliation Party (PCN). By the mid-1970s, electoral fraud at the local and national levels sent a message to the organized opposition that social and political change could not come by way of the electoral process. Widespread electoral fraud evidenced the hegemony of the military government and urged formation of popular organizations and guerrilla groups as alternative ways for achieving a democratized state.

Armed popular forces surfaced at the end of the 1970s in the climate of brutal political repression. Salvadorans not favored by the agrarian structure were aware that social change to establish democratic institutions and an end to economic exploitation depended on the combined forces of civil society. Thus, political activism required people to be part of popular organizations that were pushing to establish a democracy, even as the Salvadoran government unleashed a system of brutal repression unknown since 1932.[12] The people linked popular political organizations to armed groups for the single purpose of implementing thorough social reforms and overturning the military regime through the popular action.[13]

The government retaliated with the army, security forces, and paramilitary groups like ORDEN. The right-wing oligarchy financed "death squads," such as the Armed Forces of Liberation— War of Elimination (FALANGE), the White Warriors (UGB), and the Organization for the Liberation from Communism (OLC).[14] Political repression and murders were directed against Christians belonging to base Christian communities (BCCs). Hundreds of

BCCs developed between 1968 and 1979 with some fifteen thousand lay leaders trained in centers in El Salvador.[15] BCCs originated in the needs of the poor, who gathered to overcome personal and community problems. They fostered a historical understanding of faith in members that took root in an ethic of struggle for a better future society.

General Carlos Humberto Romero, who "won" the 1977 presidency by electoral fraud, confronted a threat from peasants who had been politicized and organized through Bible study. Church and state polarized as General Humberto Romero's regime was delegitimated by the Archbishop of San Salvador, Oscar Arnulfo Romero, who condemned government-sponsored political violence against the poor. Still, General Romero enacted the Law for the Defense and Guarantee of Public Order on November 25, 1977. For the security force, it was a "license to kill."[16] Meanwhile, international outrage soared with news of the executions of religious workers, including a death threat against the Jesuit community. Archbishop Romero grieved over having to collect the dead bodies of friends and hearing the cry of widows and orphans.

The Decline of Military Rule

On October 15, 1979, Humberto Romero was deposed in a bloodless coup initiated by junior progressive officers who hoped to avoid a revolution like the one that took place in Nicaragua. These young reform-minded officers received encouragement from the U.S. embassy, intellectuals, the Jesuits at the Catholic University (UCA), and Archbishop Romero.[17] Following the coup, a new government was formed, which selected its cabinet from the political left; however, the security force positions went to military hard-liners. Between 1979 and 1982, four consecutive juntas, based on military-civilian alliances, were established, but each successive political body moved to the right.

When the second junta was formed on January 10, 1980, following the resignation of progressive civilians, human rights violations by security forces were escalating, with civilian deaths at a level of one thousand persons per month.[18] Political repression and killings committed by members of the security forces and death squads acquired a dynamics of terror. The bodies of mutilated and tortured peasants were found each day, punctuating the Salvadoran landscape. Thousands of civilians were killed, including Archbishop Romero. Ironically, just weeks after Romero's murder, the Congress of the United States approved a $5.7 million aid package to El Salvador.

In March 1980, most guerrilla groups joined forces as the United Revolutionary Directorate (DRU). By October, all the major armed groups united to form the Farabundo Marti National Liberation Front (FMLN), named after Agustin Farabundo Marti. The FMLN drew its base from activist Christians and communists.[19] For instance, one Christian explains why he joined the revolution:

> My faith led me to join the armed struggle. I believe that God loves the poor. That is why I felt my Christian duty was to witness to the teachings of Christ. . . . I came to the conclusion that faith must be expressed in love for our brothers and sisters, particularly the poor and the oppressed. In El Salvador there is no way to escape this conclusion: the Gospel leads to a total commitment to the revolutionary struggle.
>
> Our goal is to radically transform this society. We shouldn't have to achieve this through armed struggle, but that is the only option left. We want to transform a society which produces only hunger, unemployment and death into a society which promotes life.[20]

Archbishop Romero symbolized revolutionary struggle for FMLN members, while BCCs in the rural zones provided infrastructural support and recruits. In a very real sense, revolutionary Christianity was joined to popular political struggle to counter a capitalist-oriented government that willingly and systematically slaughtered peasants to keep power. North Americans experienced the terror of El Salvador's military government when on December 2, 1980, soldiers from the Salvadoran National Guard raped and slaughtered three U.S. nuns and one laywoman, then buried them in shallow graves. Finally, the third junta was dissolved after reformist Colonel Adolfo Arnoldo

Majano was removed. Jose Napoleon Duarte assumed the leadership of a fourth junta.

Civil war was well under way when the newly installed Reagan administration declared the fourth junta moderate and centrist. Archbishop Arturo Rivera y Damas, who followed Oscar Romero as Archbishop of San Salvador, countered the Reagan administration's depiction and requested an end to military aid. By 1982, armed conflict cost between twenty-five thousand and thirty thousand lives and 10 percent of the population was displaced.[21] Between 1979 and 1982, El Salvador experienced the withdrawal of $1 billion from the economy and the bloodiest moment in national history. Structural inequities showed 1 percent of the landowners possessing 77.8 percent of the land and 2 percent of the people earning nearly half the nation's income.[22]

By the mid-1980s more than fifty thousand people had died in armed conflict and some 1.3 million Salvadorans were displaced.[23] United States tax dollars were heavily financing the civil war. El Salvador had a deficit of $241 million and a contracting economy. By 1988 the security budget consumed almost 45 percent of government spending. The national economy was sustained by U.S. economic aid. Moreover, remittances from Salvadoran refugees in the United States alone equaled an estimated $1 billion annually.[24] Finally, in March 1989, ARENA's Alfredo Cristiani, who came from a prominent coffee-growing family and was Georgetown University-educated, won the presidential election with 53 percent of the vote. His political party, the Nationalist Republican Alliance (ARENA), was founded on September 30, 1981, by former National Guard Major Roberto D'Aubuisson. Although in recent history ARENA clothes itself in moderation and reform, its ideology is rooted in nationalism, anticommunism, and capitalism.

On November 11, 1989, the largest FMLN offensive during the civil war was discharged from poor barrios surrounding San Salvador. Five days later, six Jesuits connected to UCA, their cook, and her daughter were murdered by members of the rapid response unit known as Atlacatl Battalion, organized in the early 1980s by U.S. trainers. House Speaker Thomas Foley asked nineteen democratic members of the House to form a special task force in early December, chaired by U.S. Representative Joe Moakley, to monitor investigations. Nine members of the armed forces were criminally charged, including Colonel Guillermo Alfredo Benavides, head of the military school. President Cristiani did not admit military involvement until several months later.[25]

This U.S. trained Atlacatl Battalion, an elite army unit, was involved in another massacre during the early years of the civil war. On December 12-13, 1981, it was responsible for killing over one thousand men, women, and children in the village of Mozote, in the Department of Morazán. Rufina, the only survivor and witness to that massacre, recalls:

> I believe I am the only survivor of the Mozote massacre. The village was filled with children because the people in the surrounding area had fled their homes to take refuge there. That is why the Army was able to kill so many people.
>
> The soldiers from the Atlacatl Battalion came at seven in the morning. They said they had orders to kill everyone. Nobody was to remain alive. They locked the women in the houses and the men in the church. There were 1,100 of us in all. The children were with the women....
>
> At ten o'clock the soldiers began to kill the men who were in the church. First they machine-gunned them and then they slit their throats.
>
> By two o'clock the soldiers had finished killing the men and they came for the women. They left the children locked up. . . .
>
> When the soldiers finished killing the people, they sat down and talked. I heard them say that they had been sent to kill us because we were guerrillas. I watched as they burned all the bodies. When a baby cried out from the midst of the flames, one of the soldiers said to another, "You didn't finish killing him." So the other soldier shot the baby and the crying stopped. When the flames died down, another soldier said, "They're all dead now. Let's go and kill the children."
>
> They killed four of my children: my nine-year-old, my six-year-old, my three-year-old and my eight-month-old daughter. My husband was killed, too. . . .

I spent seven days and nights alone in the hills with nothing to eat or drink. I couldn't find anyone else; the soldiers had killed everyone.

It has to be God's will that I am still alive. God allowed me to live so that I can testify how the Army killed the men and women and burned their bodies. I didn't see them kill the children, but I heard the children's screams.[26]

After the FMLN offensive, the Cristiani government and the FMLN entered into U.N.-sponsored negotiations lasting twenty-one months and culminating in the signing of a peace accord in Mexico City on January 16, 1992. The accord includes a complete plan for restructuring the armed forces and security forces, disbanding FMLN troops, and creating a new national police under civilian control. Still, the section on economic issues lacks detail. Far-reaching decisions on many economic issues are yet to be agreed upon by various groups, each of which has a slant regarding national reconstruction. Economic issues are not resolved by the peace accord, although conditions for positive discussion are introduced by it.

In June 1994, Armando Calderon Sol was inaugurated as the first postwar president of El Salvador. I was in El Salvador when Cristiani handed power over to President Calderon Sol. By then the euphoria of the peace accord was beginning to dissipate. I noticed that soldiers regularly patrol the road between the San Salvador International Airport and the capital. Some have argued that the soldiers control the rising level of crime that issued forth in the post–civil war period. Others say the military presence is evidence of the government's persistent need to institutionalize the repression of peasants. What you cannot fail to notice is the number of guns in society. Guns are everywhere. I returned to El Salvador after the new president's first year in office. By the end of April 1995, the United Nations observers left the country, although only 40 percent of the peace accord stipulations had been implemented. The post–civil war Salvadoran economy is in a disastrous state. Most Salvadorans are suffering higher levels of chronic unemployment, underemployment, and impoverishment. The new market-oriented economy is being selectively developed and it largely provides real benefits to a small business-class and the oligarchy. Salvadorans are still largely sustained by the money sent home by refugees living and working in the States. Under desperate economic conditions, crime is a widespread survival response.

In El Salvador, remittances are a major source of consumption capital. For the most part, this money is used to make investments and purchase basic goods and luxury items. A by-product of consumption capital, however, is an emerging ideology that aligns the ordinary Salvadoran with those conservative interests that seek to protect private property and capitalist investment. In part, this explains why so many campesinos supported ARENA, the party reflecting the system of government that defends the established political economy and investment structure. Ironically, Calderon Sol, who won the presidential election as an ARENA candidate, was identified in U.S. intelligence documents as having financed death squad activities in the mid-1980s from Miami, Florida.

In 1995, I traveled with a group of students across El Salvador and we met with the leader of the Nahuat people, Cacique Adrian Esquino Lisco. Don Adrian conducted a prayer ceremony prior to the meeting with my delegation. He prayed to the sun and mother earth requesting permission to enter into dialogue with the delegation of students and pastors from the United States. He talked about the *matanza* and the birth of the National Association of Native Peoples of El Salvador (ANIS). We were particularly struck when he shared that the peace accord negotiated by the Salvadoran government and the left excluded the viewpoint of El Salvador's native peoples. Land must be returned to the Nahuat people.

Faithful Witness in a Context of Violence

The ultraright defined patriotism in El Salvador by killing religious workers. Since 1972, eighteen priests, one Lutheran pastor, three American nuns, and an American church laywoman have been murdered or have disappeared.[27] Christian persecution at the hands of the military and death squads in El Salvador became a fact of daily life. The deaths of Archbishop Romero, the four American churchwomen, and the Jesuits are the most striking cases; yet, the

Salvadoran countryside is scattered with the remains of lesser-known but socially engaged Christians killed by the security forces and death squads.

As the military regime increased its persecution and killing of Christians associated with mass popular organizations, the process of formalizing belief and behavior in the BCCs involved linking the experience of death in the climate of political repression to the biblically rooted and Christian understanding of martyrdom in the service of social liberation. Thus, a new religion of martyrology arose from the climate of political repression, as common Christian interpretations made sense of political struggle in the democratic space of small Christian communities. Christians increased, "their participation in the revolutionary struggle, inspired by faith that told them 'there is no greater love than to give one's life for brothers and sisters.' "28

Thus, the Salvadoran people articulated a new religious martyrology out of their situation of political repression and economic margination. Social martyrs are symbols of the struggle of the dominated classes who seek to create unprecedented economic and political structures in the nation. El Salvador's martyrly Christianity relates belief in a God who sides with the poor and those classified "social martyrs" in the struggle to end human rights violations, while achieving the democratization of the state, the demilitarization of society, and the achievement of economic justice. These prophetic values represent a social agenda that has forged social solidarity networks in El Salvador and the international community.

The religion of martyrology denies sacred legitimation to authoritarian and repressive forms of government and the social forces that stand behind them, while requiring cultural actors to sustain a constant bond with the poor. This brand of Christian faith is a resource for political activism that seeks the structural and moral transformation of society. Faith in the social martyrs encoded an ethic of struggle, defined as laying down one's life in the political struggle for a better world. Hence, the mutilated and tortured bodies represented, to opposition groups, death for the cause of the poor. For many in El Salvador, dead peasants came to image the death of the hard-hitting Jesus who was a martyr for the poor and the cause of justice.

Social martyrs are sacred symbols formed around images of social and cultural opposition that assemble communities that contest the political state. Social martyrs permit solidarized groups in society to read their political struggle as a sacred text. Thus, social martyrs such as Rutilio Grande, Oscar Romero, the Jesuits, Elba and Celina Ramos, and the tens of thousands of ordinary Christian men, women, and children killed during the civil war, are cultural and theological productions that critique the dominant structures of a repressive regime. Martyrdom is an action blueprint that functions as a collective representation ordering social experience that demands that human beings become more human by rejecting any unjust political order.

The social martyrs focus concern on the political order as a context of cultural relations of power and domination. I have discovered, as I walked in the barrio with my Salvadoran brothers and sisters, that as sacred symbols, the social martyrs give content to the poor's oppositional ideas and behavior against marginalization from the political and economic structures of society. In the barrio, the social martyrs are important for the construction of identity and the development of social solidarity. For instance, I remember celebrating All Saints' Day several years ago in a small Salvadoran church in a barrio of the nation's capital.

Ritual in the Barrio

All Saints' Day in the life of a Salvadoran barrio community especially disclosed how ritual, articulated by the symbols of the social martyrs, gives voice to the liberative hopes of a crucified people. A cross made of cardboard was used in the worship service. The cross was covered with photographs of the four North American church-women, Oscar Romero, the Jesuits, Elba and Celina Ramos, the five young people of the church youth group *Despertar,* and images denoting the anonymous dead. By remembering those who gave their lives by denouncing social injustice and taking action against social abuses in the name of the "God of life," the past was theologically reread to serve the interests of the present daily struggle.

The cardboard cross, which was contextualized by the social martyrs, symbolized nothing other than life. Above the cross a Bible text read: "The righteous flourish like the palm tree, and grow like a cedar in Lebanon" (Ps. 92:12). At opposite ends of the cross's horizontal post it read: "To all Salvadorans who lost their lives in the last offensive, November 1989"; and, "To our brothers and sisters whose names are not known." Words at the base stated: "To the 79,000 persons murdered, disappeared, and tortured as a result of a decade of injustice against the Salvadoran people." The cross assumed by the social martyrs symbolized death so that others could have life. Martyrs followed Jesus by taking up the living cross of costly discipleship.

A large candle was placed in the center aisle of the church where members of the community met to symbolize the "light of Christ." Another large candle was lit in memory of anonymous persons such as people who were killed while working with the poor, those who were killed in the desert or river while journeying north, and the Latin Americans who have disappeared. Smaller candles were carried by Salvadoran worshipers who came to the altar with a piece of paper on which the name or names of the martyrs were written. Each person used the large candle to light the handheld one that was then placed in a tinted glass. The people wrote on small pieces of paper the names of the dead and placed these ritual objects beneath their lit candle.

After the candle lighting, the social martyrs were named exactly as follows: Archbishop Oscar Romero; the four churchwomen Ita Ford, Maura Clarke, Dorothy Kazel, and Jean Donovan; the six Jesuits and their two coworkers; the people who died at the Sumpul River and Mozote massacres; all those who died in the Spanish colonial period; the children of war; all who died for peace with justice in Guatemala and El Salvador; those who die in the States of drug-related violence and racial conflict; those who die anonymously in jails. Finally, a wooden cross was placed at the foot of the altar near the candles, symbolizing all who gave their lives for others.

I was struck by the way my Salvadoran brothers and sisters imaged the poor and their allies in social action as authentic saints whose sacrificial death in the struggle for justice symbolically negated the "system of death" ruling life in El Salvador and that system's representation in the States. From the barrio, Salvadoran refugee men and women are empowered by the memory of the social martyrs to appeal to North Americans, urging us to be instruments of peace and justice for El Salvador. Christ is risen in the barrio in the memory of the social martyrs and the practices of Salvadoran people who continue to exist in a state of permanent political struggle for life. Their sense of the living cross of a hard-hitting Jesus inspires a new life in faith.

A Lesson from God in Crucified People

Salvadorans who experienced the underside of North American economic, political, and military power declare that the American dream is a horror story. God speaks to the evils of established society in the voice of Salvadoran refugees whose demand for justice makes claims on the collective consciousness of U.S. society and mainline churches. Salvadoran refugees are speaking a word of prophecy to us. On this soil, their light discloses the reality of a crucifying global political-economic system. Their lives explain the U.S. government's promotion of injustice while referring to God's unfolding dialogue with the least of humanity. Their crucified lives are a message that condemns economic exploitation and the structures that produce poverty and death.

The Salvadoran story reflects the presence of the hard-hitting Jesus within the history of a people whose crucifixion reveals even now that they are bleeding to death in our bloodstained hands. Salvadoran refugees say the world can be more just. They ask the people of the United States who have supported the military regime to change their way of being in the world. Salvadoran refugees insist that North America's faith agenda must include a willingness to follow the revealed truth that commands the establishment of a society and international relations that deliver shalom to oppressed classes. From the barrio, Salvadorans ask mainline Protestant Christians to find God present in the struggle of those who are judged by the rich as less than human and exploitable.

The Salvadoran story says God is apprehended in the life of the strangers who enter history as agents of a new vision of humanity.

Although Salvadorans in the States remind the church universal of the Crucified God by virtue of the witness of their lives, national opinion perceives unwanted foreigners who strain social services. Indeed, Salvadorans who were in the States legally, under a program of "Temporary Protected Status" were told by the Clinton administration that they would need to return home beginning in the mid-1990s. It is far easier to eject this crucified people from the national territory than to confront the truth. Who wants to hear that the government of the United States acted sinfully toward the people of the smallest nation in Latin America?

Nevertheless, the Scriptures command us to welcome foreigners. Hebrew tradition reports that the children of Israel were refugees who fled oppressive slavery in Egypt to find freedom and a new life in another land. Mary, Joseph, and Jesus fled a murdering king and were refugees in Egypt. Jesus said, "Inherit the kingdom prepared for you; for . . . I was a stranger and you welcomed me" (Matt. 25:34-35). When the U.S. government was sending Salvadoran refugees back to face arrest, torture, and death, God spoke in the prophetic voice of refugee men and women demanding a new Salvadoran society. Some Americans remembered to "not neglect to show hospitality to strangers, for by doing that some have entertained angels without knowing it" (Heb. 13:2).

From the barrio, Salvadoran refugees ask North Americans in positions of religious and secular power: Who do you say Jesus is? What have you done to your brother and sister? What have you done in Central America? Can you see the blood of Abel in the tens of thousands dead, in the countless martyrs who cry out to the U.S. Congress, and those in the nation who willingly turn away? Openness to the particularity of crucified Salvadorans changes our world, enabling us to make a political option for the poor and socially rejected. Certainly, Salvadorans in the States evangelize the mainline church by enabling us to articulate ourselves as a people of the living cross.

From the barrio, Salvadorans evangelize the mainline church, keeping it from being exclusively influenced by a cultural process dominated by ruling elites who only wish to limit Christian social criticism and practical struggle. Our Salvadoran brothers and sisters, like so many Latinos living at the margins of North American society, remind us that the church, through the memory of its martyrs, is called to proclaim the radicalness of a gospel that is always aligned with crucified people. Clearly, the imperatives of the gospel necessitate that Christians disrupt the scandalous conditions of life that are promoted by systems of power in the world. Our Christian identity now means sharing the sufferings of Christ lived by Salvadorans in the barrios.

Salvadorans excluded from the economic and political structures of life want to build a society where "no more shall the sound of weeping be heard" (Isa. 65:19). As we look toward establishing a new church identity, let us be responsive to the needs voiced by Salvadoran sojourners and demand with them the full implementation of the peace accord, support for the democratization of society, and sustainable and equitable social and economic development. The U.S. government exported death and suffering to El Salvador throughout twelve years of civil war. Mainline churches are now in the position to promote life by advocating for U.S. aid in rebuilding El Salvador's physical infrastructure as well as its social and political fabric.

From the barrios, Salvadorans ask us yet again to join them in their struggle to find solutions for the building of a society where the majority poor will "build houses and inhabit them; they shall plant vineyards and eat their fruit" (Isa. 65:21). Certainly, the church cannot follow the lead of the U.S. government that has determined that all is well in El Salvador now that the peace accord has been signed and that Salvadorans in the States need to go home. Salvadorans tell us that the old death squads have resurfaced under the name of *La Sombra Negra* ("The Black Shadow"). The new civilian police force is also militarizing and the national budget is going to be increased on the backs of the poor majority by raising the consumer tax structure.

Mainline Christians concerned with questions of human rights and economic justice entered into solidarity with Salvadorans in the past. By seeking to renew their relationship with Salvadorans in the States, they can make a real difference in the struggle for peace with justice in El Salvador and the humanization of faith hermeneutics in the contemporary mainline church in the States. By listening to these new voices in the barrio, mainline Protestant Christians will become witnesses of the transforming power of the hard-hitting Jesus. The crucified people, whose very hands and feet were nailed to the cross by the sins of a Pax Americana, proclaim the hope and kingdom of the hard-hitting Jesus that is already present in the brokenness of history.

Notes

1. Leo Chavez, "Outside the Imagined Community: Undocumented Settlers and Experiences of Incorporation," in *American Ethnologist* 18 (1991): 257-78.
2. Alejandro Portes, "Unauthorized Immigration and Immigration Reform: Present Trends and Prospects," in *Determinants of Emigration from Mexico, Central America and the Caribbean*, ed., Sergio Diaz-Briquets and Sidney Weintraub (Boulder, Col.: Westview Press, 1991), 78.
3. See especially Segundo Montes and Juan Jose Garcia Vasquez, *Salvadoran Migration to the United States* (Washington, D.C.: Hemispheric Project, Center for Immigration Policy and Refugee Assistance, 1988); and Thomas Ward, "The Price of Fear: Salvadoran Refugees in the City of the Angels" (Ph.D. diss., University of California-Los Angeles, 1987).
4. Montes and Vasquez, p. 9.
5. A. Douglass Kincaid, "Peasants into Rebels: Community and Class in Rural El Salvador," *Comparative Studies in Society and History* 29/3 (1987), p. 474.
6. Tommie Sue Montgomery, "El Salvador: The Roots of Revolution," in *Central America: Crisis and Adaptation,* ed., Steve C. Ropp and James A. Morris (Albuquerque: Univeristy of New Mexico Press, 1984), p. 74.
7. Kincaid, "Peasants into Rebels," p. 475.
8. For a solid political history, see Tommie Sue Montgomery, *Revolution in El Salvador: Origins and Evolution* (Boulder, Col.: Westview Press, 1994), p. 35.
9. Robert Armstrong and Janet Shenk, *El Salvador: The Face of Revolution* (Boston: South End Press, 1982), p. 16.
10. Americas Watch Staff, *El Salvador's Decade of Terror: Human Rights Since the Assassination of Archbishop Romero* (New Haven, Conn. and London: Yale University Press, 1991), p. 4.
11. Ibid., p. 5. Also see Tom Barry, *El Salvador: A Country Guide* (Albuquerque: The Inter-Hemispheric Education Resource Center, 1990), p. 57.
12. Armstrong and Shenk, *El Salvador: The Face of Revolution,* p. 73.
13. Americas Watch Staff, *El Salvador's Decade of Terror,* p. 6.
14. Jenny Pearce, *Under the Eagle: U.S. Intervention in Central America and the Caribbean* (Boston: South End Press, 1982), p. 213.

15. Tommie Sue Montgomery, *Revolution in El Salvador: Origins and Evolution,* p. 103.
16. Ibid., p. 66.
17. See Tomas R. Campos, "El Papel de las Organizaciones Populares en la Actual situacion del Pais," in *Estudios Centroamericanos* 34 (372/373): 923-46.
18. Morris J. Blachman and Kenneth E. Sharpe, "El Salvador: The Policy That Failed" in *From Gunboats to Diplomacy: New U.S. Policies for Latin America,* ed., Richard Newfarmer (Baltimore and London: Johns Hopkins University Press, 1984) p. 74.
19. Roberto Leiken, "The Salvadoran Left" in *El Salvador: Central America in the New Cold War,* ed., Marvin E. Gettleman, et al. (New York: Grove Press, 1986), p. 187.
20. Scott Wright et al, *El Salvador: A Spring Whose Waters Never Run Dry* (Washington, D.C.: EPICA, 1990), p. 38.
21. Enrique Baloyra, *El Salvador in Transition* (Chapel Hill: University of North Carolina Press, 1982), p. 105.
22. Jeff McMahan, *Reagan and the World: Imperial Policy in the New Cold War* (New York: Monthly Review Press, 1985), p. 125.
23. Terry Lynn Karl, "After La Palma: The Prospets for Democratization in El Salvador" in *El Salvador: Central America in the New Cold War,* ed., Marvin E. Gettleman, et al., p. 419.
24. Ann Crittenden, *Sanctuary: A Story of American Conscience and the Law in Collision* (New York: Weidenfeld and Nicolson, 1988). Also see Montes and Vasquez, Salvadoran Migration to the United States, p. 26.
25. See Thomas Foley, *Interim Report of the Speaker's Task Force on El Salvador* (Washington, D.C.: Congress of the United States).
26. Wright, et al., *El Salvador: A Spring Whose Waters Never Run Dry,* pp. 20-21.
27. See Americas Watch Staff, *El Salvador's Decade of Terror,* p. 33.
28. Pablo Richard and Guillermo Melendez, *La Iglesia de los Pobres en America Central* (San Jose, Costa Rica: Department de Estudios Ecumenicos, 1982), p. 99. Translated by the author.

Chapter Five

Two Uninvited Guests

Shoe Repair Shops

*chanting each moment of time
the dusty day calls the blues*

*that have descended like a plague
with illness might upon our daily*

*heads in this barrio: but in the shoe
shops are found the faces of old wisdom-filled*

*men paying no mind to
sadness while enjoying the memory of*

*dear grandmothers who sang
lullaby melodies on summer nights*

*of wishing stars above. here you
could learn about the reasons*

*why the neighborhood slipped over
time into dope darkness or why the*

*little park became the Lopez family
home or about the church revival that*

pledged hope. from behind their creased
brows matured by inner cities

these shoe shine men who shout
at the busy week words that make

despairing seasons whole will
fill you with a dream that removes

all gloom if only you
dare to stop, look,

and listen. . . .

The life stories below reflect the specific historical, geographical, and political experiences of a Salvadoran man and woman.* A reader's close attention to these life stories shatters stereotyped notions of Latino life in the States as defined by welfare dependency, drug abuse and high crime, teen pregnancy, or dropping out of school. These Latinos of the barrio speak of defeating tremendous life obstacles through faith in their hard-hitting Jesus. The life stories included here are representative of the Salvadoran story. Through them the dead speak, the voiceless poor gain a hearing, and God puts forward witnesses to break historical silence. From the barrio, Salvadorans refuse to be forgotten.

Life stories are a particular variety of original speech that unifies the religious meaning of the social martyrs, the political setting and traumas of the civil war in El Salvador, and Salvadoran identity in the barrio. The life stories included here depict the autobiographical details of a man and a woman whose narrative follows the standards of memory specified by situations of suffering and oppression. Memory in the life story reflects an aspect of Salvadoran social history recalled, relived, represented, purified, and reconstructed from the context of the barrio. That is how stories of struggle and liberation make their way into popular understanding and society.

* A special word of thanks goes to my research assistant Maria Jose Pineda.

Mainline Christians who take in the details of these life stories will experience Latino cultural values and symbols as a moment of shared possibility on North American soil. The original speech that follows bids readers to enter a context where the experience of suffering and death is altered into active forms of resistance and Christian identity. The Salvadoran man and woman included in this work are both agents of a Christian culture of liberation, and representatives of human experience in society. From the sidelines of everyday life they invite "us," in their own words, to live in their cultural production of a new humanity. Their own words grant a representational quality to this work that is more forceful than my "authorial voice" alone.

Marina Takes Up the Cross

Marina is a thirty-four-year-old woman from El Salvador. She was raised in the Department of San Miguel in the rural community of Chirilagua, which is one of the regions where fighting was intense. She came to the United States through the sanctuary movement around 1986. Marina and her children narrowly escaped death. The government soldiers holding her captive were just moments from carrying out an order of execution when they were besieged by FMLN combatants. Tears often filled Marina's eyes as she narrated the experience of political repression, arrest, torture, rape, near execution, and flight from El Salvador. Her voice grew happy once she talked about coming to the United States with the sanctuary program. Marina was granted political asylum in 1989.

Marina recalls growing up in El Salvador. At a very early age she began to work with popular organizations. Then the political repression being institutionalized in El Salvador started to affect her family:

I am from Chirilagua, which is a very small community in the Department of San Miguel. I was born, reared, and studied there until the third grade. At the age of eleven, I began to work with some North American nuns who conducted Bible study with children and taught illiterate adults how to read. At age twelve, I became a girlfriend to the father of my children. By fourteen, he took me to Usulutan to live with him in marriage as husband and wife. Perhaps, I became his girlfriend because I was desperate from all the poverty and hunger that existed. He offered me a better life, but it came out worse. I am now separated from my husband and have four children.

I moved to the city of Usulutan and began working as a Communist Party activist. I had a background in community work from my own village. I had worked with priests and for organizations in the marginal communities. I visited my family every six months or once a year. My husband also worked for the Communist Party. We supported ourselves this way. Nevertheless, machismo always exists in the Latino male. Before long, I was working with popular organizations and hiding from both the army and my husband. I would leave my children with other people and go work in the countryside. I made up any lie when I returned because my husband believed there was another man in my life.

My oldest brother, now dead, returned from the States. He wanted to see me. He had been elected to political office in the village of Chirilagua. I went to see him. He told me that pressure was being placed on him by others to steal some money belonging to the village. He refused and was accused of being a communist. He said, "Well, if they call me a communist for not taking away what belongs to the people, then I am a Communist." While he waited for me to arrive, gunfire was heard just outside of the village of Chirilagua. He did not wait any longer, but rushed off to investigate. I followed close behind him and went directly to the area where he was, outside of the village.

It was the first time, around 1977, that the police, who were disguised with masks in order to pass as others, were attacking the people. We found people on the street and I asked one boy, "Why are you crying?" He said, "People with masks just finished entering the village and they ended by killing the mayor." I said, "Yes? Did they kill him?" The boy said, "Yes, they killed him. I don't know why, but your brother Salvador was one of them." I asked, "Are you sure it was him and can be a witness? Because my brother was with me talking just moments before." He said, "Yes. One of the men had the same build and told me to say when asked that Salvador B. killed the mayor."

The killer passed himself off as my brother. I told the boy my brother was not responsible and went home to put the baby to bed. I said to my brother, "Salvador, you'd better flee because they are saying that you killed the mayor." He said, "I am not going to flee; instead, I am going to see what happened. If I flee, it will appear that I did it." He went to see about the mayor. All the people looked suspiciously at him, including some relatives who wanted to take action against my family. We learned, that same day, that the police assassinated the mayor to frame my brother.

Eight days later they invited my brother to a meeting called by the dead mayor's administration. My brother always asked my father for advice. "Father, do you think it is a good idea for me to go to that meeting?" he asked. Father told him that it was a good idea to go and find out what was happening. The people were still saying that my brother killed the mayor. It was not true, not true! My brother attended the meeting and as soon as he arrived people pointed to him and said, "Here comes the mayor's assassin." After that statement was made, soldiers grabbed my brother; there were a great number of soldiers present at the time. He managed to get free and ran away.

At that time, the police were not free to shoot people in public. Salvador came back running. By the time I saw him, he was not able to even stand. He was just like the little chickens that can no longer run. Lots of soldiers were behind him and I shouted to my mother, "Mother, come and see. Salvador is running and there are many soldiers behind him!" First, he entered his wife's house, just across from my mother's house, and knocked on the door. He told his wife Marta, who was pregnant, "Marta, take care of yourself and the baby you are carrying. I will not be back. The soldiers are looking to kill me and I have done nothing."

He crossed the street to my mother's home. "Son, what is the matter?" she asked. The soldiers had lost sight of him. He said, "They are looking for me to kill me. They have accused me of killing the mayor. I didn't do it." Out on the street, my younger brother saw the great multitude of soldiers going from house to house searching. He said, "Come and see, Salva [Salvador]. Look!" It was a shocking sight. Salvador shouted to my mother, "Mother give me some water! They are coming after me!" He embraced her and left. She said, "Go this way because those sons of bitches do not know the way." My younger brother, who was twelve years old, could not stand to see his older brother flee, so he went after him.

My younger brother returned with a message for my father: "Tell Father that I will wait for him close to where he works by the rock tomorrow." We lost a brother. We knew that when you go to war you risk your life. My father went to the spot, but only found a letter. My brother asked to be forgiven for any wrongdoing. He also surrendered his children. He did not want to be a guerrilla, although he was always in favor of the people. He believed the guerrillas evolved by way of the military repression and indicated that for the same reason he had become a guerrilla. He included a few words to God, then ended the letter by saying good-bye to my father.

Afterward, they [soldiers] came to the house looking for my brother. They wanted my mother and father to tell where he had gone. Four soldiers came to look for him. Because no one was able to tell them what they wanted to hear, they threw my mother to the floor, and hit her. My father was placed on his stomach with an M-16 at his back. Mother was now sitting in a chair. My father was told to reveal the whereabouts of my brother. He told them he did not know. "You are going to die," they said. Father replied, "We are all going to die. I have not made a contract with my life. God is the only one who will decide at any given moment." They hit him.

Father cried out, "My God, my Jesus, my life and soul belong to you. If I have done anything wrong, take me away. You are the solution to everything that happens here." A soldier kicked him in the face and said, "Who are you talking to *hijo de puta* [son of a bitch]?" He kicked him in the face again. "I am asking God to forgive you. God is the only one that lives with us, the poor. God is with me right now," he said. The soldier hit him again. My mother grabbed one soldier and said, "Leave the man alone. He has done nothing; moreover, he is elderly." The soldier put his rifle to my mother's chest to fire.

I grabbed him by the chest and throat. "Leave my mother alone. She has not done anything to you. We don't know where my brother is. Does your mother know what you are doing? If someone were to question her, she would not be able to say what you are doing. What you are doing is not just. My mother does not know where my brother is." He hit my mother in the face. I could not hold back. He did not expect me to hit him. He threw me to the floor and I landed on some rocks. I hit him in the face with one. He probably thought I was weak or that I was not going to defend myself. I surprised myself since a man is considered stronger.

In 1980, my father was on his way to visit me [in Usulutan] because I could not go to Chirilagua. Because they had a son fighting with the People's Revolutionary Army and a daughter opposed to the injustices advanced by the government, my mother and father were harassed by the army. My father was often stopped in public and stripped of everything he carried. He was coming home with a chicken and the soldiers took it away. Once, my father was taken off the bus and to the mountain to be killed. My father has a great faith in divine justice. He was not killed. Someone intervened on his behalf telling the soldiers not to kill him because he was an honest person.

Soldiers were posted at my parents' home. They claimed the guerrillas used it. My parents had a great deal of contact with the church priests. The priests sent someone to listen in on a meeting [convened by soldiers]. A decision was being made about when to get my mother and father and other members of my family to kill them. They had a very long list. That night soldiers planned to come to the house for my mother and father to kill them. Mother and Father had nine grandchildren living with them at the time, the children of their children who had left for the States. A priest came and said, "Get ready immediately because we are going. If you stay, you will be assassinated within a few more hours."

My mother began dividing up the children, who would be picked up later at a predetermined place. The oldest was twelve years old. He went out with two children, one under each arm. He pretended to go out on an errand and planned to wait for my parents at a certain spot. Other people helped take the children out. The priests asked my mother whether or not she wanted to go to a refuge or go to another place. My mother decided to come to my home in Usulutan. Regrettably, at that very moment the soldiers were torturing me in my home. They took me out of the house. They broke my fingers and raped me in front of my children. They beat me and tortured my son who is now eleven years old.

They told me I had several days to vacate the house. One of the soldiers told me it was not days, but hours. Because this man warned me, they killed him. They spent the whole night watching over the house. At six the next morning, I went out with the children. I had lost all my reason. I did not even bother to dress them. They were completely naked. When my mother reached the house, it was closed. The neighbors told her that I was tortured the day before. The morning after I was tortured, a neighbor got up and gave a *colón* [money] to my children because he loved them a great deal. I did not have any money.

Marina was persecuted and pursued by the soldiers, forcing her to flee Usulutan with her children. Institutionalized violence took the form of political repression that often targeted people like Marina or was generally discharged on peasants. Ordinary Salvadorans were always the victims of soldiers' violent acts and bullets. Marina tried to leave Usulutan with her four young children in the middle of a bus strike:

The buses were on strike. I asked a man with a car to take me to San Salvador. I needed to flee that place and not look back. He drove us to the main park in Usulutan. Three men, dressed like civilians, took away his car. I was blindfolded, along with my children. I had no idea where they were taking us. The blindfold was removed at the entrance of a hacienda called the Hacienda of San Juan, which was situated in a place close to Tierra Blanca. After they took off the blindfold, I was ordered to say nothing. I had already been severely tortured. My face was completely distorted from all the beating. My youngest child began to go into convulsions. I don't know if this was related to fear, but the body temperature of the two youngest children went up excessively. The youngest child was one year old and had just started walking. The other one was about four and a half years old. Again, they saw the sexual abuse and beating that was given to me.

The soldiers kept asking me to tell them where my brother had gone. I did not know. In any case, if you tell the army the truth, they kill you or if you tell them a lie they kill you, so its better to say nothing. They said, "Well, since you do not want to tell us where your brother went, What is your last wish? You are going to die." It felt to me at that moment as if my body were floating in water. I felt that my life was worthless. I replied, "Fine, I will tell you my last wish. Kill my children first because I don't want them to be tortured anymore." The children had suffered enough emotional torture. My daughter wanted to give me a kiss before anything else, but a soldier pulled her away by the hair. She said, 'I only want to kiss and embrace my mother.' They did not permit her to say good-bye.

The guerrillas came and freed us. They captured one of the soldiers, but he escaped. In fact, all three soldiers managed to escape. When the guerrillas took control, they gave me a piece of paper with instructions for a driver to continue to safety with me. But the driver was not brave enough and he only took me and my children to the road. I was told that whenever any of their [guerrillas] people met with me, they should have a look at the paper. I did as instructed until I reached the train station in San Marcos, Lempa. The Golden Bridge that had been there was already destroyed, so when I reached that point on foot with my children, there was no transportation of any kind available that could get me across the river. Since we could not cross the bridge, we swam across the river. I found a taxi driver on the other side. Someone along the way had given me some money. I asked the driver to take me to San Salvador. I did not have any particular place in mind in San Salvador, except that I wanted to flee and not turn back. I told him, "I don't want to go back. If I return, it will be worse for me." I was filled with fear. I felt like they were chasing me and as long as I kept moving, the distance between me and them increased; however, in my heart I could still feel things.

The taxi driver dropped us off right in front of the hospital by the military quarters in San Salvador. We could not sleep there on the sidewalk. I told a man who was about to leave for Guatemala that I wanted to go, but had no money. He agreed to let me go with him. We sat on the floor of the bus. When we reached the border between Guatemala and El Salvador, I wanted to communicate with my mother. They [parents] were not in the village. My mother was already in refuge at the church of San Jose de las Montaña [Saint Joseph of the Mountains] along with other refugees. At that time, it was a place for internal refugees, refugees from El Salvador in El Salvador.

I was losing my reason because I had not noticed until we reached Guatemala and were getting off the bus that the baby was changing color. The baby was turning purple. Some woman said to me, "Your baby is freezing to death." The baby was about one year old. It was then that I noticed he did not have on any clothes. The other children did not say anything; they were not talking because of the trauma. Well, in Guatemala I pleaded with a hotel assistant to allow us to sleep in a storage room. He allowed us to sleep there, but did not want the owner to find out. I remember that the next day the children were hungry.

It was cold. I went out into the street to beg. I entered a restaurant next to the Hotel España. There was a woman who appeared to have money. She had leftover food on the table. She also took out fifty cents in Guatemalan coins and left them on the table. I asked her to let me have the food that remained on her table. She allowed me to take it. I thought the money was also placed there for me. I took the money, but it was actually for the waiter. The waiter thought I was a drunkard because I was very dirty and injured. He took me outside and hit me. He told me that drunks were not allowed in the restaurant and that I had stolen his tip.

As he escorted me out, the owner of the restaurant was just arriving on the scene. I cried out, "Señora, help me." I don't know if I felt shame or if my need from having spent four days without food or water caused me to cry out. She said lovingly, "What's wrong?" I told her of my four children and the truth, "The army is persecuting me and I have four children who have not eaten." She wanted to know what the waiter had done to me. I told her simply that he probably had me confused with a drunkard and had every reason to hit me. My body was very weak. I held on to the wall while explaining. She helped me to a table in the restaurant.

She had me get the children and made the same waiter serve us. We ate beans, oatmeal, milk, plantain, and all kinds of food. My children were dying of hunger. They ate everything. I was not feeling very hungry. I wanted to know how to get to the Salvadoran embassy to get passports. I went and they gave me passports. We boarded a bus and the person taking tickets demanded that we get off because we did not pay. I said, "I will not get off. You can force me off, but I will not get off of my own will. I don't have money, but I want to flee and go far away. When other persons get on who have paid, I will sit on the floor with my children. I will not get off."

"Get off the bus. I don't want to have to hurt you," he said. I told him, "If you must, hurt me, but I will not get off the bus." We stayed on the bus even as it made its way along the route. The bus driver and I fought all the way to the last stop. My children cried of hunger as we prepared to cross the border between Guatemala and Mexico. The bottle of milk that the restaurant owner had given me for the baby was all finished. I attempted to go through customs. I thought that passing through customs was just like going to the store. Since it was my first time out of El Salvador, I had no idea what it meant. I believed nothing would happen and it would be as simple as my entering Guatemala.

The customs agent said, "You are detained." I asked, "Why?" He answered, "You do not have any proof that you are the mother of these children. You are accused of stealing children. You will be detained until the real parents of these children present themselves." I pleaded, "I am their mother. Can't you hear that they call me Mother?" He moved me to one side. Another agent, wearing a uniform, came over and said, "Don't worry. Tonight I will help you cross the border." The children saw this uniformed one come close to me and began to scream, "Mami, don't let yourself be hit by that man. They are the ones that hit you." He told me to embrace and kiss the children to calm them down.

"What do you want in exchange for taking me across the border?" I asked. "You have to sleep with me a couple of nights. That's what all the undocumented Salvadoran women do," he said. My daughter, the oldest child, was standing next to me as the man said this. "Mami," she said, "don't go with that man. We are going to find Daddy in Mexico." I spit in the man's face and told him, "Before going to bed with you, I would prefer to sleep with a dog." At the same time, I grabbed the youngest children and ran across the border into Guatemala, where he could do nothing. The older ones came running right behind me. I was full of anger and forced by the situation to return to El Salvador.

Marina never imagined that she would take up arms to fight against the soldiers. Nevertheless, Marina returned to El Salvador. Frustrated because she was unable to find refuge in Guatemala, she became an FMLN combatant. At least 25 percent of the FMLN militia was constituted of women; many of them had suffered like Marina:

I found my brother-in-law and told him, "Here are my children. If I don't return within four months, take care of them as your own children. I am leaving to join the popular army." I felt hate toward the army for all they had done to me. I still had cuts on my face from the beating I was given. Thus, I left and met up with some *compañeras* [female members of FMLN] who took me to specific places to receive training. I told them I wanted to receive training because I wanted to fight with arms. One of the *compañeras* became a very close friend of mine and she asked permission to go with me to Tierra Blanca.

We had discovered where one of the soldiers who stripped me to have sex was living. He lived in Tierra Blanca on a poor little ranch. The *compañeras* went in one entrance. I went through the front door. The man was drinking coffee on a hammock. He turned to look at me. "Do you remember me?" I asked. He did. "If you fire, just shoot me in the arm or the leg," he said. "Now, I am the one who gives orders," I said. An old lady got up to hit me with a stick. "Leave my son alone, he is a good person and does not look for trouble." The old lady was unaware that her son worked for the treasury police. A *compañera* pointed a rifle at the old lady and said, "Señora, we do not want to hurt or kill you. Please, stop or you will obligate us to do something."

I fired a shot at the man and hit him in the arm. He fell to his knees begging me not to hurt him. I felt more anger. I remembered how they raped me. I said, "I am not going to kill you now; tell your mother why I am here." He refused to speak. I shot him again in the leg. "Tell her or you will get more of the same." He told her that I came for him because he had raped and tortured me. He admitted to having placed lighted cigars on my lips, burning my mouth, cutting my hands, breaking my fingers, and spraying a chemical in my nose that caused it to bleed. Once she knew the truth she said, "Son, it is your debt and you must pay." Then, I killed him.

I am not telling this story out of bravery. I tell it in order to show that the revolutionary army got up and won the thirteen-year-old war because the army obligated it to rise up. That same army obligated me to kill. That's why I killed this soldier for all the injustices that they committed against me. I believe that love is stronger than death. For love, one struggles and lives; for love of my children. Then, I picked up my children and returned to Guatemala. We ate from garbage. In Guatemala, my children even ate the scraps that were given over to the dogs. I begged along with my children until we reached Mexico. We lived in Mexico for some five years.

We still slept on sidewalks, under bridges, and around the market area. We ate from the garbage cans at the market, until the U.N. organization recognized me. They provided me with economic assistance and placed my children under medical treatment for two years at the Autonomous University. My children were so traumatized they would not speak. The U.N. people helped me physically, emotionally, and economically. I began working with popular organizations again and volunteered with the U.N. organization. A North American named John, working with the sanctuary movement, came to me. He asked, "You are Marina? Would you like to go somewhere else? Where would you like to go?" he asked. I told him, "Yes, I would like to go somewhere else. I would like to go to the United States where I have family."

After coming to the United States by way of the sanctuary movement, Marina and her children made a secondary migration from Tucson, Arizona, to Washington, D.C., to join family and the large Salvadoran community. She was undocumented, exploited by unscrupulous employers, rejected by her family, and left homeless in a city that saw her as just another hispanic. Contrary to the popular idea that Latinos come to the United States to live on welfare and put stress on other social services, Marina relied on no institutional support of any kind. Then, her son and husband suffered physical injuries in two separate incidents:

> We lived there until moving to Spring Road. I organized fourteen Latino families there who were being mistreated by the landlord. The roof of the building had collapsed. We still had no work, but we scraped by. I went out to walk with my children, since the weather was warm. Then, a woman was driving at a high speed on Lamont and 18th Street when she hit my son with her car. I was certain that the children were right behind me. I was already going into the apartment when the oldest child reached me saying, "Mami, they killed Bertio!" I went back to see and found my son on the ground. "Mami, I love you very much but it hurts a great deal," he said.
>
> He did not speak to me again for five days, during which time he was in intensive care. His left leg bone had broken through the skin. We took him to the hospital and five days later they told me the cost was ten thousand dollars, including the operation. They wanted to know how I was going to pay for it. I told them I would make monthly payments, but was still out of work. "Well," they said, "you have to prove that you or your husband is presently working." One woman [a social worker from a local agency] offered to find my husband work and write a letter to prove to the hospital that he was working.
>
> On Father's Day, he [husband] was coming home from work. He would go to work at 6 P.M. and return at around 4 A.M. I came home from the hospital after tending to my son. There was a knock at the door. I shouted, "You have a key, you have a key." Then, a voice called back, "No, miss, it is the police. We need your signature immediately. Your husband has been a victim of an assault and needs an operation." Some robbers grabbed him and because he only had one dollar on him they destroyed his right lung with a single bullet. Thus, the child was in the Children's Hospital and my husband was in

the other hospital just in front of it. I took turns going from one to the other.

That is the story of the United States, the story of the capital of the world. Life has treated us so severely in the States; we still have checks from companies that would pay us for work but not have any funds to cover them. We had no right to make claims against them, since we were undocumented.

Finally, Marina's own experience with suffering and oppression is related to a larger narrative of protest and resistance that enlists Christian identity and the symbolism of social martyrs to project alternative political values and behavior centered on defending human rights. Indeed, Christian faith is a cultural resource through which she is able to construct an alternative reality system that directly challenges the hopeless conditions of life imposed by living in an international system of social injustice:

> For me, to speak to the people of their suffering is equal to speaking of Jesus' own suffering at the time of his crucifixion and torture. The Salvadoran people have been crucified and beaten and they are now resurrecting. When we claim that Christ is revealed, it is because we see him in each face of those who have been tortured, in each person who suffers; and who are those who suffer? The poor. Our religion is preached out of a love for justice.
>
> Christ who died on the cross is the one who is revealed in the tortured and the peoples that suffer. In the Bible, it says that they went to Herod to announce that the king of kings was born. Herod said that there could not be any other king but him. The followers of Herod disguised themselves as clothes merchants to look for the king [Jesus], the king of justice. The king of money was Herod. I compare this story to the death squads who enter people's homes to kill them under various disguises. Thus, Christ is revealed in every human being who suffers.

The God who sojourned with our mothers and fathers speaks in the voice of this Salvadoran woman. She is an uninvited guest who reveals the face of Jesus and brings a new word from God that indicates how to restore the deepest principles of American democracy. She utters a prophetic cry from the barrio that aims to deliver a shattering blow to North American ignorance and social indifference:

> Christianity is not demonstrated in this country [United States]. A Christian nation would not have supported the Salvadoran military with millions of dollars for so many years. In El Salvador, we could have built schools with that money. I would have loved to have been a student, but had no access to education. There were no schools or money for me; yet, the North American government was sending some two million dollars daily for bombs and all that. I do not consider this to be a Christian act. I am not referring to the whole country, but to the higher levels of society. Those who have been in solidarity with us—they are the Christians.

Wetback Dream

*a dream hurried wetbacks from
villages where stones tell
of massacres and death.*

*they come reproving the people
who make truth to print in papers
that murder history with neat*

*published lies. a dream
took them across borders and
rivers to come and live in cities*

*where people do not care to
see Latino faces picture God
as insignificant and standing*

against sin. with a dream
they climb to the roof at
night with waiting eyes fixed

on the dark sky for a sign
to burst open with good news
burning their ears of life

no longer underneath the
stomping feet of those better
off. a dream of not aching

in this land so savage to
the rejected. a wetback dream
from a people who never dry

their tears complaining troubles
to God and hope for better days

for us. . . .

Evangelized by His Word

Ramiro is a thirty-six-year-old man from a small rural community in the Department of San Miguel. He grew up poor but completed ten years of education. He left El Salvador in 1980 after Archbishop Romero's murder. Since coming to the United States in 1986 with the sanctuary movement, Ramiro has done solidarity work to support the cause of the poor in El Salvador who seek an end to war and the demilitarization of the nation. Ramiro told his life story to North American communities about death squad massacres he perceived to be supported by U.S. tax dollars. Ramiro believes Salvadorans living in countries scattered around the world increase others' awareness about the civil war in El Salvador and the system of life they left behind.

Ramiro shares a two-bedroom apartment with four others. His room has posters on the wall that name the United States as the source of injustice and oppression in El Salvador. One poster showed a row of dead bodies beneath which appeared the words, "A Kinder Gentler Nation, Not a Dime for El Salvador's Death Squads." Another poster produced by a North American solidarity group read, "Stop the War from the Middle East to El Salvador." An image of the Virgin Mary and Jesus on the cross hangs on one of the walls; a large flag of the United States, which he explains was a gift from a North American family whose house he once regularly cleaned, hangs on another wall. Living as a refugee has meant being stuck midway to nowhere—the plight of uninvited guests.

I am from *canton* [village] Tierra Blanca of the jurisdiction of Chirilagua, San Miguel, El Salvador, Central America. My adolescence in El Salvador was different from those who live in the city. The life of those who live in the *cantones* is different from the city where they have all the institutions built up such as schools, churches, hospitals, and markets. I was raised in the *campo* [country] where life is typified by husbandry and agriculture. In the first grade, I went to school by walking a distance of three kilometers from my home to a *canton* called *El Progresso.*

I finished my first and second year of study in that village. Afterward, I went to school in a town in the jurisdiction of Usulutan and studied until the seventh grade. Because there was no higher grade of study in that school, I had to transfer to the city of San Miguel to attend my eighth and ninth grade. I did not have enough money to finish my studies, so I had to seek the help of my sister, not so much of my father, and go to the capital of El Salvador. There I went to a government school that did not cost money to attend. Once there, I started my *bachillerato* [high school] in business administration. I only completed my second year.

I also took classes at the seminary of San Jose de las Montaña [Saint Joseph of the Mountains] on weekends and during weekdays whenever I had extra time. I began, at this time, to serve the people and to have a more direct presence among the poor, to help them. I could not return for my third year of school because of a death threat from either the White Hand or UGB, which are members of the death squads. The death threat came because I was in direct agreement with the movement of the FMLN and the just fight of the people. They were fighting for the majority of the people who do not have a plot of land for their home, and lack communication, electricity, hospitals, and schools.

There are many illiterate people in the country and others who have much knowledge. The government is opposed to mass education because they fear the people will rebel if educated. But with or without education, the people are rebelling. The people are getting up. I organized neighborhoods and villages for the revolutionary movement in our republic. The authorities suspected I belonged to the guerrillas, but I never feared death. I do not fear death, for Jesus demonstrates that he was the principal revolutionary member and was persecuted for a just cause in order to leave us in peace and the land without borders or owners.

I thought it was my responsibility to make a contribution to the movement of the people. That's when the threats began. I received a sheet of paper under my door from the White Hand. I was living with my sister at the time, but she was not aware of what was happening. I remained for a little time in San Salvador. I slept in many different homes and went into hiding. I finally went to the seminary, San Jose de las Montaña, to Archbishop Romero and Sister Ita Ford [one of the church workers raped and killed December 2, 1980]. They advised me to stay in hiding in other homes and churches until they resolved my problem.

They planned to help me study, although *bajo de agua* [clandestinely]. They wanted me to prepare to serve the Christian communities and the poor in the rural or agricultural zones. They were going to give me a scholarship to study in another country, but that was when Archbishop Romero was killed, and all the papers were lost. His files were destroyed or stolen by the army. Our seminary had often been attacked and people taken, but they never found photos of me. If they had found a photograph of me, I might have fallen into the hands of the army quickly. Perhaps, this saved me.

I felt torture in my own flesh. Soldiers did not batter me or capture me, but I had a bullet in my head. I also had a bullet pass through my left side when we guarded the body of Archbishop Romero at the Metropolitan Cathedral in San Salvador. Three of my friends were tortured by the [Salvadoran] National Guard. They were taken by the neck and thrown onto the ground, then beaten with rifle butts and kicked. They were left like Christ dripping blood, then were thrown into an ambulance. This ambulance was not of the people; it belonged to the military service. I don't know what happened to those souls. Surely, they were probably killed and buried and are now among the disappeared.

For me it was very difficult to get out of El Salvador. I had to sleep in the mountains for five days and in the homes of some friends that I trusted. I had no money to pay for transportation. My parents were not aware that I had to leave the country. They ignored the groups I belonged to; only my oldest sister in San Salvador knew what was going on. I told them [parents] that I was going to Guatemala as a tourist. I never told them the truth. They asked me how long I would be away. [I said] Three days to buy tires for a motorcycle.

I did not ask my mother for any money. I was filled with anxiety and felt like the world was coming to an end. I felt like crying. I was told by friends that on the road I planned to take there were three army guards. I knew it would be necessary to take that road. I prayed as Romero had taught me. I was on the bus praying. After the bus reached the guards, I got off and went to the mountains to avoid being searched or being asked for papers such as a visa or passport. I did not have papers. I only had my sister's address in San Salvador and my name on a piece of paper.

I left El Salvador at 5 A.M. The war curfew was still in place. I left my valued things behind; not anything of great wealth, but the work with my brothers, sisters, parents, and my studies. I had no idea when I would return to study; what I had always desired was to be a professional. I was going to another land where I did not know anyone. I thought Where will I live? In what home? I will be like the bird that goes from tree to tree; going from continent to continent. Yet, Jesus Christ existed in this manner in his day as well.

I had lots of medicine like aspirin for the headache I was experiencing. I had three pairs of pants and three shirts. After getting past the guards in Guatemala, I made contact with friends from the University of San Carlos. I had been there before for a talk and had made them aware that one day I would have to emigrate. They paid for my hotel. I was there for a whole night. I felt fear because the Guatemalan and Salvadoran armies collaborate. I had to leave at nine in the morning to catch a bus for Mexico. Several bombs went off close to the hotel where I was staying.

Of course, this was not strange to me. I had just come out of a context of war; I feared being hit by a stray bullet. If that happened, I would die and my parents, relatives, and friends in the struggle and at the school would not have any word from me. When I got to the Mexico-Guatemala border, another noble friend and his acquaintance met me. My friend told me not to go by the guardhouse; rather, they gave me passage beneath the guardhouse in a river whose water came up to my waist. I was very hungry and thirsty. I drank the water from that dirty river to quench my thirst. After coming out of the mountains, these men took me to a house in Chiapas. I felt like a free dove; free of oppression and the fear that I would fall into the hands of the enemy.

I lived in Mexico from 1980 to 1986. I truly felt spiritual support in Mexico when a Salvadoran brother asked how many days I had been in the country and where I was living. I told him three days and that I was living underneath a bridge. I indicated to him that I had the address and name of a Mexican friend but could not find him. He told me not to feel alone, that I could return to his home with him. He also said that the next morning we could visit some friends to find out how to adjust and find work. At that point, I felt like part of a family; like I had found another brother related to my very mother and father.

I went to his home. It was satisfying not having to live on the street, being protected in a home. We went to his friends' home where I met a group of Canadians, Australians, and Americans. From them I received food, clothing, and an orientation concerning the situation of refugees there [Mexico]. Little by little, I became aware that these friends were working for the just cause of our people, that is, the struggle of our people.

I worked with the refugee community in Mexico, taking care of visa transactions for Salvadorans, Guatemalans, and Nicaraguans. I felt happy and satisfied in Mexico because it was not like being in another country; I felt as if I were at home. We are people that speak the same language and understand the same situations. Well, I could not stay in Mexico for health reasons and because I wanted to help [economically] my parents, brothers, and sisters. The North Americans told me I had to emigrate to the United States to work with Central American refugees.

I left in 1986 after communicating with the sanctuary people in Tucson, Arizona. The sanctuary people of Tucson, Arizona, told me I had to come and work with the refugees. At that time I was very ignorant of life in North America, especially in terms of how to survive. In light of this ignorance, I asked whether all life in North America is capitalist. They said it was not all capitalist. They came to get me. I felt a sense of loss on having to leave the first place that I came to know as a refugee: Mexico. I thought my words to my friends were coming true about living like a bird from tree to tree.

North Americans from the sanctuary movement came for me to take me across the border. It took three attempts to get over the border. I spent much time waiting in the Sacred Heart

Church of Aguas Prietas. When I first attempted to enter the church at Aguas Prietas, the priest kept me out. I told him that the house of God is never closed to a refugee. The priest insisted that I could only enter with a reference. No one knew me. I told him that I was a Central American refugee and was sent to that address to wait for certain people. "What are their names? How do they look?" he asked.

One of my contacts used a cover name so it was difficult to answer. I had to figure out how to communicate with the brothers in sanctuary in Mexico in order for them to talk to this man [the priest]. When he did not accept us (I had another person traveling with me) that first night in the church, we slept in the park. We were afraid in that park because there were many people who wanted to hurt us. Then, we talked to the priest and he told us that a call had come from Mexico. He gave me a bed for the wait.

On my first attempt to cross the border, at two in the afternoon, Kathy [with the sanctuary movement] came to pick me and several other persons up. We left Aguas Prietas for the border, but could not cross it. Immigration was everywhere: in helicopters, with dogs, on horseback, and in cars. She said it was not a good time to cross the border. We turned back and went to the church. The following week we made a second attempt. Still there were too many patrols. Her car broke down, too. She returned to Tucson. The following week on the third try we crossed the border. A pastor who was on the border informed us that there were no patrols and the time was right.

We crossed and went to his house. Two cars were waiting for us after the crossing. I felt less fear with these people. I did not feel at risk. The brothers said, "Ramiro, welcome to the United States." They embraced me. For me, this was very painful and I had to cry and look back. I wanted to look at what I had left behind. I left behind my home, my family, and my studies. I was even studying in Mexico and I had no idea when I would return to my studies. I was in the workers' university in Mexico. I was studying to be a catechist, as well as studying politics and medicine. I also did social work for the community. Again, I was cut off from what I desired for myself and my people.

In Tucson, I was taken to the home of a North American friend who spoke very little Spanish. They were concerned that Immigration would come searching houses. We were advised not to talk. We spent the first three days out of sight. Then, we did a television interview at the University of Arizona and in the sanctuary church. We gave testimony about the reasons for coming to the United States, what was happening in our country, and that they [North Americans] had to give sanctuary to the many more who would have to emigrate due to *la situacion* [the situation]. Sanctuary was promoted this way for the purpose of protecting the human rights of Central American refugees.

I recognized from the beginning the good intentions of these people and am very grateful to them. They made connections for me with Los Angeles. In Los Angeles, I gave testimony in Plaza Olviera. They already had my name, photograph, where I was coming from, and the kind of work I did. In Los Angeles, the people were better informed than were the people in Tucson, Arizona. I did not have any place to live [in Los Angeles], but they found me a room in Casa Grande. This Jesuit-run house is found in Hollywood. Sanctuary, in the form of housing, food, orientation, and connections with people to facilitate survival [work] were given to any refugee who arrived.

Sometimes it's hard for others to realize that those of us who fled the violence of El Salvador, those of us who live outside— the refugees—are also combatants of a kind. We leave for other lands and nations to give testimony and learn how to fight for housing, against hunger, and for the needs of others. We learn to orient others regarding their papers, work, hospitals, and housing. People do this for one another. When our people return to our country for the reconstruction, they will not say they found no one to support and orient them. On the contrary, they will testify that they got to the United States, Canada, Australia, Holland, or Mexico, and always found a *compañero,* a brother.

In early 1987, I came to Washington, D.C., as a participant in the second refugee sanctuary march [sanctuary testimony circuit] that was organized by CARECEN, *Ayuda* [Help], CRECEN, and Casa del Pueblo. The Methodist, Catholic, Baptist, and Episcopalian churches connected with the sanctuary movement were also involved. I gave testimony intended to let people know what was going on in my country in its twenty-seven states. Well, this is how I came to Washington [D.C.].

North Americans always asked, "Why did you leave El Salvador?" I responded, "You who are in this supposedly powerful country, but whose power is in money, How would you feel living under bullets when you had no idea where they were coming from or going? What would you have to do to get out of that country that was in war, especially after being threatened with death? How would it be to leave and have to live on the streets with nothing to eat? What would it be like to go out into the street afraid that you would not return alive at the end of a day? Fearing that you would become disappeared or return home dead?"

In our country the guerrillas do not exist. What does exist is the rebellion of a poor people against the rich and against a military regime. In my own flesh, I suffered the bullets that afflict the people. I absorbed the air of bombs, not pure air. I gave them this testimony and showed them the bullet wounds. I urged them [North Americans] to form base communities to go to our republic to see the consequences and to experience in their own flesh the noise of bullets and bombs. They would then say, "You are right. I would have left as well to save my life."

I would tell how the people do not have education, medical service, electricity, or ways of communication; I stopped going to school because I did not have the money to buy books; my parents could not pay for my schooling. Books were so expensive. This was also part of my testimony to the North American people. In our own flesh is seen the presence of Jesus Christ, and North American listeners are participants, through refugees, in that flesh. During this caravan, I was given the homilies and a photo of Archbishop Romero in order to remember our leader who watched over human rights in our country and in the whole world. Well, this is how I came to Washington, D.C.

Refugees living outside of El Salvador help unfold peace. I think the role of refugees is the most important in a war. If refugees did not come out of the country, people would simply say that in El Salvador there is war but only words would be heard; only news would be heard. But the countries of the world have become aware that El Salvador is at war because people have left with physical damage. These people have given testimony of that war and shown the injuries they have received. All of this has caused the United Nations to take notice of the refugees. Refugees are a people of El Salvador who have had to leave their country to ask for peace.

Ramiro, who worked mostly as a janitor after reaching the United States, engaged in union organizing. Because his lungs were damaged from working with toxic chemicals, he has been unemployed and living on disability compensation.

After the sanctuary march, I stayed in Washington and got a job washing dishes in the Sheraton Hotel. I earned $4.75 an hour. I covered all my expenses, from taxes to medicine for my health, with this salary. Once I left that job, I went into custodial work cleaning buildings. I organized a group of workers in the building to protest the company that was exploiting us. Three hundred fifty Salvadorans ended up without work. I found the location of the union that was to organize them and I received their support. I unionized eight buildings. That was the job I had until this day. Now, I am unemployed.

Ramiro's God-consciousness links personal identity to a Christian commitment to work for social change. Ramiro speaks to us, informed by a faith understanding that uses the Bible and Christian symbols to make a critical commentary on social relations and to portray what are considered meaningful aspects of social reality. For Ramiro, God, Jesus, and the social martyrs symbolize the struggle for justice that negates the social system approved by those who rule:

In 1980, I was preparing for my final exams in my second year of study for the *bachillerato*. I heard over the radio, JSAX, the Panamerican Voice of the Church, that Archbishop Romero had been killed. They announced that for the next two hours there would be silence in memory of Archbishop Romero. When I heard this, I felt like the ground had opened up and was swallowing me as well. I am very thin, but it felt like my flesh came off.

Archbishop Romero was a great minister and someone to respect. When I mention him it is like seeing him and feeling him. For me, he is not dead. He was a spiritual leader and someone to orient me toward life. He captured the sentiment of the Salvadoran people. The force of his own spirituality, his courage to live with tuberculosis sufferers in the hospital, his fearlessness in confronting the situation of the country even though it led to death; these same things happened in the time of Christ. I could say right now San Romero de las Americas [Saint Romero of the Americas], not Archbishop Romero.

I was hurt by Romero's death. He was unjustly killed. He simply told the military and the government the truth concerning what was happening in the country. The government, high military leaders, and the U.S. government believed that by killing Romero the guerrillas would stop. Romero was taken, but the movement continues its struggle. Everything did not end with his death; and they [ruling forces in society] are not going to continue in power. To this day, they have not been successful, and Archbishop Romero lives in El Salvador and in every refugee body all over the world.

The deaths of the Jesuits affected me a great deal. Their deaths were also seen as a productive seed. The deaths of the Jesuits helped the Salvadoran people expose the real assassins to the light of day. Now the people and the whole world are aware that it is not the guerrillas [FMLN popular army] that kill religious; instead, it is the *militares* [military forces]. Their deaths moved the church to pressure the United States Congress to give temporary papers allowing refugees to enter the United States [Temporary Protected Status or TPS]. Although their bodies have died, their spirits and energy live on in El Salvador and in the church of the poor in Washington.

Christianity is tied to the poor and the root paradigm of martyrdom:

Christ was poor, persecuted, and assassinated. Christ was poor in terms of power on earth and money, but not of spirit and belief. The mission of the church is to make the rich know that the poor have a spirit that is richer than those who are materially rich in money and land. The thought of the church of the poor is not like that of the rich who think only of a rich Christ, and not in a poor Jesus. So this is the concrete message the church of the poor takes to the rich: they should share their wealth with the poor. The rich should not live off the poor.

The poor tell the rich, "Yes this leader existed and struggled. He was tortured and killed." Today, this Jesus gives liberation to the poor. The world that the church of the poor is going to construct is one where all the nations on all the continents will construct lands without frontiers, without divisions or discrimination between Black, White, and tan. On the earth, there will not be anyone denied the right to exist. The church of the poor signifies that there should be union and harmony in everything; without laws or big politicians who disgrace human beings. Thus, we are to be liberationist in all things or what some call in other words "liberation."

The church of the poor practices the Bible. The Bible is a code that our ancestors left for our time. Many people have taken it to do business, and use it to make people ignorant. There are many little groups; I don't know what they are doing, but it's a pity that they walk around carrying the Bible and respect it but they are not even aware that this very book tells them to come out of their ignorance. In the Christian communities, the Bible motivates the people. It gives them an additional medium of expression and way to touch the heart of the rich, the capitalist.

The poor are making their mental liberation by showing that they no longer have to be tied to the old biblical laws. They are constructing a modern Bible. In our country, they are creating a new Bible—a real New Testament, as Archbishop Romero called it—based on the New Testament and what the people are living, on what has happened. We will create the Bible of the Americas. It will contain the themes of the old Bible and the events that have occurred and will happen in the future. This Bible will help others who are still repressed by their leaders in governments such as in Africa, Asia, and in other countries where no one preaches the liberation of God.

For Ramiro, the Bible is both a crucial faith document containing the narrative description of God and a tool of political consciousness. As for many of the new Central American Latinos of the barrio, Ramiro looks to the Bible for reports of the history of liberative struggle made by God against unjust social systems imposed by those who control the material means of life. Ramiro's testimony suggests that Christian communities need to commit themselves to building social relations based on equality, democracy, and human rights. In his testimony, death is imaged as structural injustice and institutionalized violence, while the life sacrifice made by those who follow the social martyrs is believed to lead to the end of exploitation and social injustice.

The Stone Rolled Away

The martyred speak in the voices of a Salvadoran man and woman whose faith recounts the experience of stones rolled away from untold tombs. In these life stories, the received Christian tradition as represented by the Bible—standard symbols such as the cross, or specific understandings of Jesus—are given subversive power in relation to particular social contexts of oppression and social disregard. Through these barrio-dwelling brothers and sisters, the people whose lives were crushed by the weight of political injustice say Salvadorans expect security, equality, and humanization in their lives. Surely, North American Christians will agree that all God's children should have work, know a just peace, and be treated as human beings.

As I opened up to the evangelistic moment of the Salvadoran community in the United States, it has become quite clear to me that statements about the existence of God are rather meaningless in the context of cold, social reality. In the barrio and ghettos, we know that a forced religious commitment inspired by church-based assertions of God's existence fails to address the harsh reality of death fostered by oppressed conditions of life and widespread violence on the streets. Marina and Ramiro remind us that faith in God is only verified by worldly action that produces a more human and liberating reality for people. Christians are those who act as persons who have passed out of death and into life to love and toil for others (1 John 3:14).

The life stories included here may well be seen as a moment in God's truth. Indeed, more attention needs to go to Latinos who read their Bibles, aware that Jesus was not a man who closed his eyes to the problems of reality. Jesus confronted the problems of everyday life as well as the injustices corresponding to the social forces delivering oppression to the poor. If we listen to Salvadorans and other politically committed Latinos in the barrio, they tell us that genuine Christian witness means responding to the world of those who suffer inhuman poverty and sinful violence. Undoubtedly, our journey of obedience leads us away from the idea that faith is a private matter devoid of meaning in the concrete situations of men, women, and children.

More than ever, mainline Christians need to reread the Bible and their social history from the perspective of those whose lives have been trampled by social forces that idolize wealth and power. The God of the Bible approached history in solidarity with the oppressed and acted in society on their behalf. Latinos, such as those whose words were recorded above, point out that in a world where so many are condemned to existence at a subhuman level of life, it is scandalous to reduce Christianity to hearts strangely warmed. The gospel is not an evangelical emotion but good news worked for the poor and burdened. Mainline churches must seek to accompany the poor and outsiders on the long journey that alters society for the common good of all creation.

Latinos are surrounded by broken bodies in their communities in the States and in Latin America. The spiritual values that find representation in Latino lives invite mainline churches to see and hear crucified people criticizing societies that create conditions of wretchedness and death. On the faces and in the testimonies of the people of the barrio, Christians rediscover that God does not permit oppression to go unanswered. Latino newcomers assert that God frees people to struggle for a better way of life. Indeed, real liberation is generated in the process of struggling for a new type of political organization, social development, and economic empowerment.

Marina and Ramiro are the voices of a Christian movement whose international following is certainly part of a larger critique of what is wrong with profit-oriented society. From them we learn that the memory of suffering is both a hermeneutical resource for interpreting the Scriptures and a vehicle for organizing protest and resistance. Through a people's memory of suffering, individual experience becomes a useful tool for judging and criticizing political injustices with a vision to reconstructing social reality. North American race, class, gender, and ethnic social movements have also used their memories of suffering as a powerful source of vision for organizing the politically disempowered and socially marginalized.

Clearly, mainline churches need a new vision of church that requires personal faith to be understood in light of the larger social reality in which people exist. Interestingly, the life stories describe a powerful belief system that shows lowly and crucified people finding strength in God and the will to make a historical difference for their society. Taking up the cross means walking up to the tomb of the hard-hitting Jesus, confident that the stone has already been rolled away by a God who puts life into all those situations that only offer anguish and death. In the barrio, Latinos like Marina and Ramiro suggest that the cultural role of mainline churches is to shape and amend their culture in response to the work of God in human history.

Mainline churches in the States can discharge this historical role by feasting with uninvited guests who are kept isolated from mainstream society, yet presuppose the reality of God (Luke 14:15-24; Matt. 22:2-10; 25). Our brothers and sisters in the barrio call upon mainline Christians to develop congregations as instruments of a sacred love that renews the world of people left for dead on the side of the road. What kind of a church is needed to respond to the urgent matters faced by crucified people? Does the church meet the anguished cry of people like Marina, Ramiro, and so many others nailed to crosses with silence? Let us explore answers to these questions in the next chapter.

Chapter Six

The Uninvited Guest

Busy Winter Street

twisting breezes on the dusty
street pause on our block almost
listening to the pentecostal preacher

talking about the meaning of repentance
in otherworldly ways while condemning
the dispossessed for sins in deed committed

by an uptown world to them. on another corner
of this inescapable place the neighborhood
is gathering to watch the children in their

dance of hope while forgotten by
the joy this brings are the heatless nights
of winter the landlords force upon us to

raise profits another fraction off
all shivering backs. over there is
la bodega where all the old men play

dominoes talking about drunken mothers and
fathers who never hear the preacher or
see the children dance dreams the image

of laughter for all the street to know.
yes, it is a very busy street that others
seldom visit and God has merely passed

along the way. . . .

Mainline Christians find themselves in a very peculiar place in their denominational lives. Church leaders wonder what needs to be done to improve the ministry of their congregations. A swarm of pastors and laypersons are attending workshops that offer the latest techniques on new pastoral methods and church growth approaches to revitalization. Surely, few would argue against the current search by mainline Christians to understand the task of the church in the world. Of course, some are acting on the belief that salvation is only guaranteed by the church. Others hold that a deeper examination of God's deeds in human history will yield a new way of thinking about the church's mission in the present.

All this activity must surely mean mainline Christians are ready to rethink the meaning of the church. People in the pew, concerned to establish an authentic Christian identity for the next century, are raising deep theological questions about the role of the church in the divine/human encounter. How in this conflict-ridden world is the church a sign of the union of God to human beings? Some church leaders answer this question by becoming friendlier with the social gospel aspects of their denominational traditions. They emphasize the practical service of the church in the world. Progressive leaders argue that if the church is a visible sign of salvific history where God performs mighty deeds, then the church must certainly seek life in the world.

In the world, God meets the anguished cry of humanity in all places with good news. That means mainline churches need to bear witness to the gospel of God, "the mystery that has been hidden throughout the ages and generations but has now been revealed to [God's] saints" (1 Col. 1:26). More than ever, we must be prepared to reclaim the idea that God's redemptive action in the world intends to create a new human community. In the many situations in which men, women, and children find themselves, the church—which was born in the power of the Spirit—is sent to work compassion on behalf of all humanity. Today, such basic service is especially imaged by feasting with the uninvited strangers who are never wanted at the table of mainstream society, despite being favored by God (Matt. 22:2-10).

As mainline churches reinvent themselves, they will need to embody the true meaning of the good news of Jesus by walking with the poor and social outcasts in ministry. A church that sits at the table with uninvited guests discerns the way God is revealed in the lowly and those at the margins. When the mainline church allows itself to be inhabited by the real world of uninvited guests and enacts its faith in critical relation to economic and political structures, it will face political dangers for the sake of the gospel. Mainline Christians proceed on the road paved by their hard-hitting Jesus by understanding how food, healthcare, housing, social opportunities, and human dignity are linked to the presence of God in the world.

Rethinking the meaning of the mainline church means mobilizing new pastoral energies based on a faith that critically confronts everyday situations secure in God. Mainline churches functioning as agents of the good news of the hard-hitting Jesus always declare that their mission is not bound by geographical, social, economic, racial, ethnic, patriotic, biological, cultural, or political borders. Instead, they reclaim the mission of Jesus as imaged by the New Testament images of community. Hence, the church is the people of God serving the goals of salvation, the historical body of Christ oriented to the world to come, the dwelling place of the Spirit, and an institution made distinct by tradition and polity from other forms of organized social life.[1]

For too many mainline Christians, the church is no longer the historical and spiritual expression of a hard-hitting Jesus. It is a social club or psychotherapy group. Yet, the revelatory character of the social misery of places like the barrio insists that mainline churches stop ignoring the hard-hitting Jesus' call to become incarnate in the world. Mainline churches are to lose their present life in order to find it in the flesh and struggle of society's neglected people who hope in the gospel. In other words, "those who want to save their life will lose it, and those who lose their life for my sake, and for the sake of the gospel, will save it" (Mark 8:35). Hence, discipleship now means not only loving all persons, but especially the suffering poor who are always left out.

Modeling the life of the hard-hitting Jesus needs to be a goal of the institutional presence of the mainline church in history. This means confronting the power structures over people that cause oppression and dehumanization with the intention of changing them. Awareness of the brutalizing aspects of social reality deepens Christian faith in God who, on the cross, knew the meaning of social cruelty, unjust suffering, systemic poverty, and alienation from main-stream society and institutions. Mainline churches eager to find new identity are now called by the uninvited guests of the barrio who are already at the banquet table celebrating the resurrection of the Crucified God. It is time to find the hard-hitting Jesus who lives with outsiders.

Toward a Theology of Ministry

Mainline churches are community-based institutions responsible for bringing together the sacred beliefs and practices of people to shape individual Christian identity and moral community.[2] As embodiments of the church universal, congregations are the primary instrument for bestowing Christian identity on persons. They provide individuals with a sense of community by offering growth in faith and support in times of crisis; they establish social links in people's place of residence and beyond; and they nurture an ethic of service within and outside of the immediate faith community.[3] Congregations need also remember they are narrative communities where people are called to recollect and act on stories about God who loves uninvited guests (social outcasts).

One place to see the uninvited guests is the barrio. For the most part, mainline churches have too often played the role of minimizing internal doubts about the functioning of U.S. policy in relation to the poor of the barrio. In particular, mainline churches have largely not defended the structural concerns of the barrio with strong conviction. Moreover, Latino mainline churches also have been less socially conscious of their more powerless Central American brothers and sisters now living in the barrio and fleeing civil war and economic destitution. Mainline churches bearing witness to the hardhitting Jesus need to remove the missional blindness that keeps Christians from the people of the barrio.

In the barrio, uninvited guests place an emphasis on the church serving oppressed humanity. Interestingly, the people of the barrio have been left out of the mainline churches' new awareness of the importance of listening to the redemptive message of the once-muted cry of wretched humanity. In the barrio, Latinos speak of the church through their existential experiences of pain and their theological interpretation of the faith. Who listens? These uninvited guests tell members of dominant society that the larger cultural system convinces people they can never have too much power, too many possessions, or too much pleasure. These rejects of America's banquet tables remind the church to be ultimately preoccupied with building a society free of racial and economic oppression.

In the barrio, Latinos believe too many mainline churches have become mere liturgical centers for hearing Sunday sermons that lack credibility in the world. Although organized social ministry is quite low on the priority list of these churches, God's Word needs to be enacted in the service of the battered and expectant reality of the barrio. The gospel's message is not about maintaining inwardly turned mainline churches; rather, it requires churches to discover Christ in the local barrio already renewing people's minds for the creation of a church turned to the world with a message of salvation. Churches facing the world find their identity in activity that lets "justice roll down like waters, and righteousness like an ever-flowing stream" (Amos 5:24).

Certainly, Christians gather for worship around the Word of God to shape and strengthen their identity. Although in recent years mainline churches have centered nearly all of their worship experiences on the concerns of the individual, worship now needs to give shape to ministries with uninvited guests. The Word that gives rise to Christian identity in worship is a better reflection of discipleship when congregations serve people made invisible in society. Worship ought to reflect the hard-hitting Jesus. Any relativizing of the suffering and death marking the life of Latinos and Latinas based on a generic idea of salvation denies this Jesus who turned the cries of uninvited guests into a living hope and said to followers, "apart from me you can do nothing" (John 15:5).

The church begins with the resurrection of Jesus of Nazareth. Hence, the church whose roots are in the promise of life is always to be a sign in history of the truth and love of God. The risen Jesus died for his solidarity with poor and uninvited guests. He leads the church for the sake of oppressed humanity in need of redemption, and oppressors in need of conversion. Today, bearing testimony to Jesus means accompanying people who are rejected from the banquet tables of a moneygrubbing society. Indeed, theologies of ministry that place the barrio's uninvited guests at the center of their ecclesiology bear witness to the identity of the hard-hitting Jesus. Such a starting point for ministry makes the church good news for ignored people.

As congregations gather for Bible study, worship, and to celebrate the sacraments, they acknowledge the revelation of God-in-Christ. Yet, this visible community needs to be in ministry precisely where the risen Christ is already hidden and waiting to be found: with uninvited guests. Mainline churches will restore meaning to their identity when they recall the gospel's requirement to identify with the barrio. Discovering Jesus in the barrio, hidden in the sick, poor, imprisoned, homeless, hungry, downtrodden, undocumented alien, and underemployed, negates the idea that solidarity with disdained people is optional for Christian ministry. The true church knows it works for justice on behalf of the least of humanity (Matt. 25:31-46; James 1:27).

Any theology of ministry concerned with the downtrodden will include a proclamation witness not afraid of giving testimony to the life, death, and resurrection of the hard-hitting Jesus. This means mainline churches will give testimony to the word of life made manifest, seen, and proclaimed over time (1 John 1:1-2). The hard-hitting Jesus indicates that the word of life must be fearlessly announced amid the structural injustices and institutionalized violence that comprises the human experience of the rejected people of the barrio. Mainline churches defending the rights of the poor through words and acts will thereby help to organize the power of the poor into an instrument for the overcoming of dehumanizing systems of domination.

Although dominant society continues to practice injustice in relation to the barrio, biblical anthropology says Latinos are made in the image and likeness of God (Gen. 1:26-28). In the context of the barrio, to be a Christian means condemning the sin that destroys the life of those people considered insignificant, and promoting full humanity. Because Jesus told the disciples when the church was founded "you will be my witnesses" (Acts 1:8), a concrete commitment to the barrio requires bearing witness to the gracious love of God that embraces its people. Any new identity for mainline churches must include a readiness to suffer affliction for the work of denouncing injustice and proclaiming the gospel of the God who is with us (1 Thess. 3:3-4).

For years, mainstream religious and secular institutions have expressed an *odium justitiae* (hatred of justice) toward Latinos living in the barrio. Nonetheless, mainline churches approaching the hard-hitting Jesus, who always take the way of the lowly and uninvited guest, hear from the lips of the barrio poor that God "will swallow up death forever" and "will wipe away the tears from all faces" (Isa. 25:8). Once they share the oppression and suffering of those who live as uninvited people in society, mainline Christians will find ways to challenge the materialism of a U.S. society that erodes community-based values, creates barrios, and bolsters an identity of social indifference.

A theology of ministry not only orients itself by the ministry of the hard-hitting Jesus, but it maintains that the church is fundamentally a community of compassion and unrestricted love for others. Historically, there are ways to refer to the various ministries of the church that contribute to a better understanding of how Christian identity functions in the world. Christian identity gets exercised in the church through the marks of the church's ministry of *koinonia* (fellowship of love and solidarity), *kerygma* (bearing worldly witness to Jesus' Lordship), *diakonia* (gospel-motivated service to crucified people), and *martyria* (suffering persecution and even death for defending the poor, strangers, the dispossessed, and oppressed).

In recent history, the Latin American church has suffered martyrdom for defending the rights of the poor and unmasking sinful structures. The ministry of *martyria* exposes the consequences of sin in the world. This ministry holds that genuine Christian identity comes from responding to the world of those who suffer inhuman poverty and political oppression. Offering one's life for the cause of the poor reflects witness to God. Finally, a theology of ministry is incomplete without *dikaioma* (historical action that issues forth in partial realizations of divinely mediated peace with justice). *Dikaioma* demands that human beings become more human by announcing and working for a new social order where the poor and uninvited guests find justice with peace.

The true church does not meet the anguished cry of people who live in the societal junkyard with silence but with *dikaioma* ("a just action"; cf. 2 Cor. 9:8-15; 1 John 3:10; Rev. 22:11), which practically assures ultimate conditions of communal well-being (cf. Isa. 32:15-18; Ps. 72:1-4). Can it be that mainline churches are called to be a sacred space of justice with peace in the barrio? Churches that see the need to tell the story of God's saving acts in history engage in *dikaioma* in the barrio to draw nearer a new society of freedom, justice, peace, respect, and equality. To be sure, embodiment of this form of ministry means seeking to eradicate economic injustice, hunger, alienation, xenophobia, violence, and other systems of anti-life.

One way for mainline churches to deepen their theology of ministry is by actualizing these marks of the church, beginning with the formation of a small cultural-awareness-for-ministry reflection group of about twelve persons. The purpose of this group is to both deepen the congregation's understanding of culture as the context of theological identity as well as to clarify the ministry of the church relative to places like the barrio. Because anthropology takes a holistic approach to the human being, the cultural-awareness-for-ministry reflection group will benefit from looking at the human being in terms of various scientific models of group and individual life.

Thus, as the cultural-awareness-for-ministry reflection group moves toward clarifying its theology of ministry and enactment of the marks of the church already discussed, it may enlist the model that follows. Because this model interrelates social and natural science perspectives of the human being, understanding of what it means to be a human being in any social context will be enhanced. Each member of the group will have the task of identifying a set of articles from a scientific model of the human being to be shared with the reflection group. As the various models of the human being are related and inte-

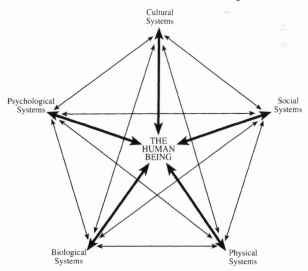

The Holistic Nature of Anthropology

Anthropology seeks to discover the interrelationships between various scientific models of the human being.

grated into a holistic picture, members of the reflection group will then want to ponder the implications for the church's theology of ministry.

What Christians learn from the holistic model of the human being is that culture is the context of people's lives and larger social, economic, political, biological, and psychological factors play a role in the meaning system of a community. Christian life always takes place then in the time and space of different cultures. The universal value of the gospel is always in the process of acquiring cultural embodiment. Awareness of this very important cultural fact leads to the renewal of mainline churches that think they are incapable of looking differently at the world (Rom. 12:2). The reflective process outlined above will offer a new framework for faith that does not seek the triumph of one way of life and identity.

The cultural-awareness-for-ministry group must also bear in mind the characteristics of culture as it establishes a link with people in the barrio. For instance, it must be noted that culture is not genetically programmed into human beings; instead, it is a socially acquired system of meaning for interpreting experience and generating behavior. Culture provides social groups with a coherent set of symbols, values, attitudes, and explanations about the world, individual identity, and social life. People use their culture to successfully adapt to their physical and social environment. And finally, culture is always changing, is experienced differently by members of the same group, and is a critical ingredient of group solidarity.

God Revealed by Uninvited Guests

One of the dinner guests, on hearing this, said to him, "Blessed is anyone who will eat bread in the kingdom of God!" Then Jesus said to him, "Someone gave a great dinner and invited many. At the time for the dinner he sent his slave to say to those who had been invited, 'Come; for everything is ready now.' But they all alike began to make excuses. The first said to him, 'I have bought a piece of land, and I must go out and see it; please accept my regrets.' Another said, 'I have bought five yoke of oxen, and I am going to try them out; please accept my regrets.' Another said, 'I have just been married, and therefore I cannot come.' So the slave returned and reported this to his master. Then the owner of the house became angry and said to his slave, 'Go out at once into the streets and lanes of the town and bring in the poor, the crippled, the blind, and the lame.' And the slave said, 'Sir, what you ordered has been done, and there is still room.' Then the master said to the slave, 'Go out into the roads and lanes, and compel people to come in, so that my house may be filled. For I tell you, none of those who were invited will taste my dinner.'" (Luke 14:15-24)

In church, people nurture their spirituality, live in community, and find answers about how to live in the world. Many laypersons tell their pastors they go to church to find a truth that will help them to be better persons. Certainly, people want to meet Jesus in the Word preached and in the social interaction of their congregation. They don't want to feel indifferent toward the image of Jesus proclaimed from the pulpit. Neither do people in the church want to find a Jesus so removed from their reality that they could reject him. The story of the great banquet lets us meet once again a hard-hitting Jesus. Jesus reminds us here that those who are poor and uninvited to the table of the well-to-do reveal "the kingdom of God and [God's] righteousness" (Matt. 6:33).

Routines of daily life such as eating and drinking are taken for granted in modern society. Most people hardly take time to consider how these activities suggest the frailty of the human condition or have sacred meaning. Meals are occasions to create community with others; they are also events of estrangement and separation. The ministry of Jesus included eating with sinners, tax collectors, hungry masses, as well as with the well-off. For Jesus, eating and drinking was an important time to reveal the redemptive presence of God that was especially extended to the social outcast. In fact, Jesus' mealtime practices with the despised both broke the mainline religious rules governing eating and induced opposition from ruling authorities.

In the gospels, eating and drinking have theological meaning in the ministry of Jesus. Jesus often ate with others (Mark 2:15-16; Luke 7:36; 10:39; 11:37; 14:1; 19:5-7). He often invited people to eat with him (Mark 14:22-23; Luke 15:2; 24:30-31). He was known to enjoy meal sharing to such an extent that he was accused of being "a glutton and a drunkard" (Matt. 11:19; Luke 7:34). Doubtless, table talk with the disciples was one basic context for Jesus' teaching about the meaning of God's reign and the ultimate fulfillment of life in a new community in God (Mark 2:17; 14:6-9; Luke 7:36-50; 10:39; 11:39-41; 14:1-24). Although eating with Jesus does not secure salvation (Luke 13:26-29), meal sharing foreshadowed life in the kingdom of God (Luke 15:23-24, 32).

Members of the Jesus movement did not fast as was common of other religious groups of the time (Mark 2:18-19). Meal sharing was not only a time to celebrate the inbreaking of God's reign in the daily life of people, but it was also a way to issue a powerful critique of a religious viewpoint that disallowed God's acceptance of all human beings. Jesus' disciples did not fast; rather, they ate with outcasts precisely because they knew that for poor people who never get invited to anything, fasting was not a practical act. People who have enough to satisfy their hunger are in a position to fast as a form of religious discipline. When you have plenty to consume, giving up food for a particular period of time is not hard. The destitute who mostly know daily hunger do not fast, however.

The poor are not thinking of fasting to express their relationship to God; instead, they cry out to heaven for food and justice. Indeed, the uninvited guests spend time wondering how to put food on the table to sustain their lives. Fasting, for those who suffer on the margins of society, is a ruling-class religious observation whose conventional theological wisdom denies the basic structures of social injustice and economic inequality that cause hunger and want (Isa. 58). If fasting is a private practice that people with plenty to eat can engage in without thinking of why others go hungry, then Jesus' practice of eating and drinking with social outcasts and the poor are acts of solidarity imaging the community of love God wants for us.

In the story of the great banquet, Jesus' teaching on eating and drinking are simply expressed. If the ministry of Jesus revealed God to human beings in a ministry that released captives, offered sight to the blind, and declared that liberated existence begins by following

Jesus, then in the story of the great banquet Jesus focuses attention on the persons who likely did not fast but searched daily for food: social outcasts. The story is easy to follow. A man planned a dinner party, and invited people of high social standing to it. The original guests made excuses for not attending the banquet. Then, the householder commanded that the poor, maimed, blind, and lame be invited. Because there was still room, strangers and outcasts from the highways and hedges were urged to come.

The beginning of Jesus' story stated, "Blessed is anyone who will eat bread in the kingdom of God!" These words draw us into the simple plot that uses table fellowship to speak of the already present activity of God. The story also makes us wonder about the cast of characters. A host wished to have a big party. What do we know about him? Was he a social climber trying to gain status by giving a party for the wealthy elite? Did he want to show off a new place? Did he invite marginalized people out of anger at the urban ruling class who in turn refused to come to his party? We are left with many questions about the host of the dinner party, yet, unexpected people were certainly welcome at his table.

The initial guests made excuses for not coming to dinner. Surely, we have made excuses to avoid God's call to fellowship. What is the meaning of the original guests' excuses? What does it signify that they gave up their place to strangers and outcasts? Consider the original guests. Their excuses made sense in the context of the property concerns of the rich whom they represent in the story. The first of the three excusees was likely an absentee landlord who declined the dinner invitation due to the purchase of a field outside of the city. The second excusee was also a landowner who bought five yoke of oxen— a sign that he owned a large amount of land. Then, the recently married man invoked family obligations to avoid the banquet.

The excuses seem to come from respectable people. The original guests said no to the dinner invitation to attend to property, possessions, and family. Many people who are "decent" church folk could probably identify with these concerns. Yet, it was obvious that the banquet was prepared for more than just these three guests. Although the initial guests may have stayed away because they were able to satisfy their own hunger and had other concerns, one can imagine they stayed away after hearing the man invited outcasts to dinner. Cultures operating out of a purity system organize society around polarities of clean and unclean, insiders and outsiders. The unexpected guests were those considered by the purity system of the then-Jewish social world as unclean.

The unclean, such as the abjectly poor, the physically ill, and outcasts were separated from "decent people" (those who observed the purity code). In Jesus' story the social elite would have declined the dinner invitation disfavoring participation in a meal that equally included the unclean or outcasts of established society. Doubtless, the first guests were probably pious Jews who acted in terms of the cultural codes appropriate to their understanding. Because the uninvited guests were considered part of the dirtiest level of society, fellowship with them in the intimate setting of meal sharing defied standard wisdom.

Jesus' story attacks the purity system when table fellowship takes the form of radical inclusiveness. The kingdom of God does not operate on the basis of a language of difference and the practice of exclusion. In this story, Jesus aimed to criticize the purity rules of how to prepare food, what to eat, and with whom. Those rules make the poor voiceless in society. I suspect the original guests were advocates of the purity system. They stayed away because the riffraff of the barrio and social margins were coming to dinner. Jesus, who negatively images "decent people" who are members of the upper classes, approves of the action of the host. The host invited strangers and outcasts into a community of mutual acceptance. He opts for "unclean people." Table fellowship begins to give life for those most threatened by systems of denial and death.

What does the story of the great banquet tell us about God's will for humanity? It tells us God wills life for people, especially the poor and outcasts who exist in universes of sorrow and oppression. From the standpoint of ethics, the story does not suggest involvement in the life of outcasts simply because those who live at the margins are present and growing in numbers in society. The great banquet calls persons to discern the character of a God who is especially revealed by social rejects. The uninvited guests raise a basic question about the character of God. Faith in God is not a private possession to be expressed after other things are out of the way. Instead, faith means answering yes to God who favors social nobodies.

In Jesus' story "full humanity" means living for the God who is revealed in situations of human ruin, and sharing the struggle and hopes of disdained people. Surely, the uninvited guests likely knew a scandalous situation of misery similar to that now known by most people in the world. Generally, those who are voiceless and uninvited to the table of "decent people" suffer from mass unemployment, underemployment, forced migration, lack of education, poor health-care and housing, sickness, hunger, and premature death. God does not withdraw from the ugly sides of the human condition nor does God approve of ways of thinking that separate people from one another; instead, God calls us to the side of suffering humanity to begin a feast of fellowship.

Turning our backs on the situations of brokenness so familiar to uninvited guests actually separates us from God. God who is visible in the human form of Jesus knows what it means to be socially reject-ed and broken (John 1:18; 3:11; 12:45; 14:9). In the story of the great banquet the harsh situations of the human condition are not avoided nor is worldly wealth given a divine blessing. In the story there is no option made for the well-off; instead, the story thrusts us into situations of pain in the wastelands of society to find God. Because "Christ Jesus . . . emptied himself, taking the form of a slave" (Phil. 2:5, 7), and "though he was rich, yet for your sakes he became poor" (2 Cor. 8:9), God is found in the barrios' streets and lanes and in the hedges and highways.

Through Jesus, God promises to make a feast for us in the midst of the trials and toils of daily living. Still, the "decent people" of the church often prefer not to relate to unclean strangers and poor peo-ple. "Good-for-nothing" poor people are not invited to table fellow-ship. Not surprisingly, Christians often reproduce debates in the public square that lean toward declaring that those who struggle to survive deserve exclusion from mainstream society since their pover-ty reflects their lack of contribution to the creation of wealth. Those defined as social outcasts are said to have no regard for personal responsibility and the work ethic (an ideology that supports the exploitative relations that create prosperity for some and misery for most).

Certainly, notions about social outcasts are molded in the cultural context of society, which sets the boundaries of people's belief and behavior. Capitalist culture produces purity rules that call some people undeserving and keep most people blind to social reality.[4] The poor, homeless, strangers, the chronically ill, and disabled are not only blamed for their plight, but both liberal and conservative talk about them rarely touches on larger issues of politics and power. Popular understanding—a mixture of ideology and politics—largely ignores that economic restructuring increases the ranks of the poor, U.S. policy overseas pushes people toward the States, budget cuts remove safety nets for the ill, and public policy helps enlarge the marginal groups in society.

In the conventional wisdom of capitalist culture, people are judged valuable insofar as they are economically productive to a profit-oriented society. Any good observer of the rules of purity in capitalist culture, then, will find virtuous qualities in those who display great wealth and will look at poor persons as those who simply burden society by living off the resources paid for by others. To be sure, dominant cultures' conventional purity system constructs the identity of the poor (especially of the barrios and slums) as a group of people in permanent undoing, a collection of individuals who have morally failed a money-oriented society, nobodies to be kept in "otherness." Yet, this cultural attitude of exclusion (cleanliness) is not the way of Jesus.

The story of the great banquet speaks directly to people who seek to minister to those who hold these views. Christians can look to society's sense of the uninvited guests and challenge it from the perspective of the gospel, which says the predicament of the poor requests neither rejection nor scorn. Discerning God's reign revealed in the story of the great banquet means refusing to accept the dismissive judgment of a society that tolerates and promotes the want and misery of the barrios and slums where uninvited guests live.

Churches in ministry to the wider culture proclaim that those who live on "the streets and lanes of the town . . . the poor, the crippled, the blind, and the lame" suffer age-old injustices.

Doubtless, this parable was told to convey the good news of God's grace and forgiveness that encircles all people, especially neglected people who too often feel hopeless. The people of the barrio and the poor who are judged worthless by the larger society are those who respond immediately to God's offer of friendship and new community. Clearly, Jesus' story is about the church becoming a community of good news that includes poor and outcast men, women, and children. As a messianic community, the church must remind those focused on the security of family, property, and full stomachs that from the barrio to El Salvador the uninvited guests who suffer the most wish to engage in table fellowship that issues forth in redemptive community and action.

Jesus' story of the great banquet is about overcoming barriers to authentic community. Ultimately, Christ, who is the host of the dinner, asks us to overcome our own boundaries of race, ethnicity, gender, class, and culture. For an affluent society such as the United States, one boundary to overcome is the inability to see the world from the perspective of the radical other at the margins of so-called respectable society. Nonetheless, accepting Christ's invitation to the great banquet means undergoing the experience of entering a new world, that of the ignored people in the nation's barrio whose actuality has never been of concern in the world of mainline churches.

Certainly, mainline churches serving the interest of the more affluent subdivisions of society will hear a special message in this parable. As host of the great banquet, Christ overturns the logic of affluence that narrowly centers on the logic of private wealth that is consuming the world and leaving people and the earth scalded by its evil. The good news of the great banquet is that God loves a party and wills life and approval for all people. God prepares a table of friendship for the uninvited guests in the barrio. Rich and poor. Male and female. Black, White, Brown, Yellow, and Red. All are invited to table. God calls us to be one people. Only in this witness of radical inclusivity will the church be a new community in the world.

Embodying the gospel in this way will enable the church to bring down the dividing walls of hostility in society to make the world a better place.

Notes

1. Orlando Costas, *The Church and Its Mission: A Shattering Critique from the Third World* (Wheaton, Ill.: Tyndale House, 1974), chapter 2.
2. Emile Durkheim, *The Elementary Forms of Religious Life,* trans. Joseph W. Swain (1915; reprint, New York: Free Press, 1965).
3. Robert Wuthnow, *Christianity in the Twenty-first Century: Reflections on the Challenges Ahead* (New York: Oxford University Press, 1993).
4. See especially Michael B. Katz, *The Undeserving Poor: From the War on Welfare to the War on Poverty* (New York: Pantheon Books, 1989).

I. Theological and Biblical Studies

Diaz-Isasi, Ada Maria. *En La Lucha/In the Struggle: Elaborating a Mujerista Theology.* Minneapolis: Fortress Press, 1993.

Gonzalez, Justo. *Mañana: Christian Theology from a Hispanic Perspective.* Nashville: Abingdon Press, 1990.

Greenway, Roger S. *Discipling the City: A Comprehensive Approach to Urban Ministry.* 2nd ed. Grand Rapids, Mich.: Baker Book House, 1992.

Gutierrez, Gustavo. *The God of Life.* Maryknoll, N.Y.: Orbis Books, 1991.

Herzog II, William R. *Parables As Subversive Speech: Jesus As Pedagogue of the Oppressed.* Louisville: Westminster/John Knox Press, 1994.

Kaylor, R. David. *Jesus the Prophet: His Vision of the Kingdom on Earth.* Louisville: Westminster/John Knox Press, 1994.

McKenna, Megan. *Not Counting Women and Children: Neglected Stories from the Bible.* Maryknoll, N.Y.: Orbis Books, 1994.

Recinos, Harold. *Jesus Weeps: Global Encounters on Our Doorstep.* Nashville: Abingdon Press, 1992.

Sobrino, Jon. *The Principle of Mercy: Taking the Crucified People from the Cross.* Maryknoll, N.Y.: Orbis Books, 1994.

Williams, Delores. *Sisters in the Wilderness: The Challenge of Womanist God-Talk.* Maryknoll, N.Y.: Orbis Books, 1994.

II. Sociology and Anthropology

Augenbraum, Harold, and Ilan Stavans, eds. *Growing Up Latino: Memoirs and Stories.* Boston: Houghton Mifflin Company, 1993.

Canada, Geoffrey. *Fist, Stick, Knife, Gun.* Boston: Beacon Press, 1995.

Devine, Joel A., and James D. Wright. *The Greatest of Evils: Urban Poverty and the American Underclass.* Hawthorne, N.Y.: Aldine de Gruyter, 1993.

Handler, Joel F. *The Poverty of Welfare Reform.* New Haven, Conn.: Yale University Press, 1995.

Hunter, James Davison. *Culture Wars: The Struggle to Define America.* New York: Basic Books, 1991.

Kottak, Conrad Phillip. *Cultural Anthropology.* 6th ed. New York: McGraw-Hill, 1994.

McGuire, Meredeth. *Religion: The Social Context.* 3rd ed. Belmont: Wadsworth Publishing Company, 1992.

Muller, Thomas. *Immigrants and the American City.* New York: New York University Press, 1993.

Sharmin, Arvind, ed. *Women in World Religion.* New York: State University of New York Press, 1987.

Takaki, Ronald. *A Different Mirror: A History of Multicultural America.* Boston: Little, Brown and Company, 1993.

Wuthnow, Robert. *The Restructuring of American Religion.* Princeton: Princeton University Press, 1988.

4138625R10095

Made in the USA
San Bernardino, CA
31 August 2013